Inklings

ON PHILOSOPHY AND WORLDVIEW

A new way of learning
about our connections
to Truth & Reality

Tyndale House Publishers
Carol Stream, Illinois

Visit Tyndale online at www.tyndale.com.

TYNDALE and Tyndale's quill logo are registered trademarks of Tyndale House Publishers.

Inklings on Philosophy and Worldview

First edition published in 2010 by WheatonPress.com. Fourth edition published in 2017 as *Inklings on Philosophy & Theology* by WheatonPress.com under ISBN 978-0692229934. Fifth edition by Tyndale House Publishers, Inc., in 2020.

Designed by Jennifer Phelps, with much assistance from Lindsey Bergsma

Edited by Jonathan Schindler

For information about special discounts for bulk purchases, please contact Tyndale House Publishers at csresponse@tyndale.com, or call 1-800-323-9400.

Names: Dominguez, Matthew, author.
Title: Inklings on philosophy and worldview / Matthew Dominguez.
Description: Fifth Edition. | Carol Stream : Tyndale House Publishers, Inc., 2020. |
    Includes bibliographical references. | Audience: Ages 13-18 | Audience: Grades 10-12
Identifiers: LCCN 2019031265 | ISBN 9781496428967 (trade paperback)
Subjects: LCSH: Christian philosophy. | Philosophy.
Classification: LCC BR100 .D59 2020 | DDC 261.5/1—dc23
LC record available at https://lccn.loc.gov/2019031265

Printed in the United States of America

26   25   24   23   22   21   20
7   6   5   4   3   2   1

For my students: "A thousand thanks."

For my future students: "To the breach!"

To all of my family and friends who have helped make the
impossible possible in Christ: "Here's to water walking!"

To the next generation of water walkers: "Further up and further in!"

TABLE OF CONTENTS

You will know the truth, and **the truth** *will set you free.*

JOHN 8:32

See to it that no one takes you captive through hollow and deceptive philosophy, which depends on human tradition and the elemental spiritual forces of this world rather than on **Christ**.

COLOSSIANS 2:8, NIV

Don't copy the behavior and customs of this world, but **let God transform you** *into a new person by changing the way you think. Then you will learn to know God's will for you, which is good and pleasing and perfect.*

ROMANS 12:2

But in your hearts revere Christ as Lord. Always be prepared to give an answer to everyone who asks you to give the reason for the hope that you have. But do this with **gentleness and respect**.

1 PETER 3:15, NIV

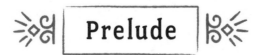

Prelude

I trust you will find the information on these pages helpful on your journey.

As you peruse the bits of material dappled here and there, it is important to keep in mind:

The daily decisions we make in life are based on our conclusions concerning the nature of reality.

Everyone is trusting.

The only way we live, eat, sleep, move, communicate, and eke out an existence is to make decisions based on whatever we consider trustworthy.

As long as humans have engaged in conversation and shared ideas, we have differed on the object of our trust, our faith, our belief, our confidence.

Most philosophers agree that Plato and Aristotle's works on the true nature of reality are a foundation for all human interaction, and although epic cultural shifts have ensued . . . races and religions have been defined . . . empires have risen and fallen . . . every individual continues to make every single decision based on whom and what he or she trusts—as true, as real, as *worthy* of trust.

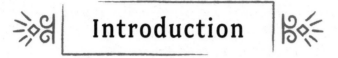

Introduction

The Birth of Christ is the eucatastrophe of Man's history.
The Resurrection is the eucatastrophe of the story of the Incarnation.
This story begins and ends in joy. It has pre-eminently the
"inner consistency of reality." There is no tale ever told that men
would rather find was true, and none which so many sceptical
men have accepted as true on its own merits.

J. R. R. TOLKIEN

We all have to pick a story to help us make sense of our world. The story we choose to trust frames our day-to-day realities. Erwin McManus, an insightful pastor in California, says that in our competitive, media-packed modern culture, "whoever tells the best story shapes the culture."[1] He goes on to say that often the truth is lost in bad storytelling, and falsehood is spread through a well-told story.[2] I think this has been true for humanity ever since the earliest story times around warm, intimate fires.

We all live a life of faith. And consequently, we all live our lives trusting in one story or another. Furthermore, as we trust these various stories, transmitted from generation to generation, creatively invented or adapted, unconsciously consumed or intentionally adopted, we often forget that these tales are human attempts to explain the inexplicable and to comprehend the incomprehensible. More importantly, we often forget (or deny) that these stories are theories. They are our best attempts to get it right. We all want to know what is really going on in the universe, and our stories—our worldviews—are the distilled essence of our collective efforts to describe what is really real, what is truly true, what is worthy of trust.

My approach to worldview and philosophy is simple and practical. It builds on and extends the ideas of the iconic works of Socrates, Plato, and Aristotle on the nature and consequences of our beliefs regarding Prime Reality. In essence, these brilliant minds helped us see that the spiritual (the nonmaterial) and the material are the two basic elements for the fabric of reality. From this foundation I propose there are four basic story lines available to humanity:

+ **Idealism** trusts that only the spiritual/nonmaterial world is real.
+ **Materialism** trusts only in the reality of the measurable realm of matter.
+ **Monism** trusts in the unified existence of the spiritual and material realm as one gigantic entity.
+ **Theism** trusts the reality of both the spiritual realm and the material realm but maintains an understanding of real unity and real distinction between the two.

In this book we will study these four main options in conjunction with the ways they answer several of life's essential questions. We will also see how these four options point to the fullness of Christ in a life-giving, Christ-centered worldview. Doing this will give us clarity about and awareness of our own views and those of others, and we will begin to see how our objects of trust have shaped our personal choices. This knowledge will empower us to make intelligent and informed decisions about the multitude of religions and "isms" available to each human and to engage in honest, honoring dialogue with those whose views are different from our own. And we will also see how the truth found in all worldviews points us to the truth found in Christ. As Augustine says, "Let every good and true Christian understand that wherever truth may be found, it belongs to his Master."[3]

As you read this book, study these ideas, and examine your own choices with new understanding, my hope is that your personal story will be shaped and changed. This book has the potential to impact your life in a significant way that may then change the rest of your story.

Before I give a brief overview of this book, I need to make my position very clear. It is essential for all people to have freedom and dignity to choose their personal beliefs, and I want this book to create a safe and healthy forum for exploration and authentic self-discovery. I have no desire to create a weak, insufficient, or biased description of another worldview in order to sway your opinion or manipulate your decisions. Rather, I want you to have a greater sense of self-awareness and ownership not only for what you choose to believe but also for why you believe what you believe in the context of so many options.

However, it is also important to note that particularly the last part of this book is an overt, unashamed invitation to my readers to learn more about Jesus Christ as the fullness of reality. In my years of teaching philosophy to students at a Christian high school, I have shared the four main worldviews again and again, and I have each time come back to a quote by G. K. Chesterton. In his book *Orthodoxy*, he writes, "They have torn the soul of Christ into silly strips."[4] As I teach my students that each worldview is but a portion of the truth—though we trust in the worldview we hold to as if it were the whole—I am convinced that the fullness of truth and reality are found only in the undivided person of Christ. The story I choose to believe as the true story holds Christ's birth, incarnational life, sacrificial death, powerful resurrection, and bold commissioning as its centerpiece. This center provides the main plot for the entire story of human existence—an unfolding drama we are all in. I believe all great stories point toward this greatest story and invite us to awakened and intentional participation in it.

Therefore, the last part of this book speaks to those who want to learn more of what it means to see Christ as the center of history or who are interested in what authentic Christ-followers believe. I understand this does not describe all readers. If you are not interested in trusting Christ at this moment on your journey, I hope this book enables you to see why other people do choose to trust him. Either way, this book should clarify your understanding of the major worldviews available to humans and also offer a fresh perspective of the grace and truth found in the person of Jesus.

I grew up striving to be worthy of the apostle Peter's call to "always be prepared to give an answer to everyone who asks you to give the reason for the hope that you have" (1 Peter 3:15, NIV). I worked hard to be prepared to defend my trust in Jesus. Unfortunately, I was not actually living out the call as Peter originally wrote it. I was working in order to gain others' approval, which I was convinced would elevate my value as a human being. I worked from a desire to be recognized and loved; I cared more about my public image than about the impact I had on the people around me. I learned painfully late in my journey that 1 Peter 3:15 *actually* says, "Always be prepared to give an answer . . . for the hope that you have. But do this *with gentleness and respect*" (emphasis added). The apostle Paul compels us to do everything with love or our efforts will amount to nothing. Without authentic love for others, my words and actions are merely a "noisy gong or a clanging cymbal" (1 Corinthians 13:1).

How does this truth apply to our study of worldview? Choosing a particular belief system—any belief system—without incorporating love, gentleness, respect, and honor will do you and the world a disservice. On this journey, it is essential to treat all people with dignity and respect. Christianity sometimes has a sour reputation for being abusive in this global worldview discussion. Unfortunately, we are known for trying to be right at any cost instead of being known for showing love at any cost. The apostle Paul knew what that feels like, and two thousand years ago, he set the standard for Christ-followers: "While knowledge makes us feel important, it is love that strengthens the church. Anyone who claims to know all the answers doesn't really know very much. But the person who loves God is the one whom God recognizes" (1 Corinthians 8:1-3). With those words in mind, the approach to examining worldview described in this text is based on a foundation of love, honor, and dignity, and it supports the use of grace and truth as we interact with others.

THE STRUCTURE

This study of worldview is divided into three parts.

In part 1, we will examine the common denominator of *trust*. No matter which worldview we follow, we are trusting something. Everything is based on trust. The only way we live is to make decisions based on what we consider trustworthy, though we differ on the object in which we place our confidence. We give authority to what and to whom we trust, and it is essential for us to understand that every decision we make is based on our conclusions regarding the nature of reality.

In part 2, we'll look at the four main worldviews in which humans place their trust and how each of these answers some of life's essential questions. Idealism, materialism, monism, and theism each hold a portion of the truth, and each provides those who trust it with answers that influence how they live. Here I am neither endeavoring to exalt any one worldview above another nor setting each up only to knock it down. I want us to examine each one with as unbiased a view as possible.

Regarding the subject matter presented in part 2, I deal with only four basic views in their purest forms for two main reasons. First, this text is intentionally not a text on comparative religion or a grocery list of isms (there are plenty of those). This text is concerned with how to use the specific lens of philosophy to think critically about what we trust and particularly *why* we trust what we trust. This lens not only gives us a fresh look at what we believe; it also empowers us to understand why others choose to believe what they believe. Second, addressing only four basic views makes it manageable for us to learn about the particulars of our trusted beliefs in the context of other beliefs. Many writers have found other excellent—though more complex—ways to study and teach world religions, isms, and comparative worldviews, and I have been inspired by several of these authors, including C. S. Lewis and James Sire. The simpler philosophical approach offered in this book is not antithetical to these texts; rather, this book should serve to enhance your access to other approaches.

Part 3 puts the "silly strips" from Chesterton's quote back together and examines Christ as the fullness of reality. The truth from each of the four worldviews is put together, seamlessly, in Jesus Christ. We often work so hard to make our one strip of Prime Reality into the entirety. We stretch it to make it fit every question or issue or reality we encounter, but only in Christ do we find both complete truth and complete grace. And only in the power of paradox do we find the freedom and integrity to live in harmony with the life-giving tensions and apparent contradictions implicit within Prime Reality.

A companion volume to this text—*Inklings on Christ-Centered Biblical Discipleship* (2021)—will examine what embracing the tensions of the paradoxes of Christ looks like practically in a life following his. This text—*Inklings on Philosophy and Worldview*—is about the various stories humans tell about the world and themselves; the companion text *Inklings on Christ-Centered Biblical Discipleship* looks specifically at what it means to find ourselves in the grander story, the "true myth" as Lewis calls it,[5] of what God is doing in the world through Jesus Christ and in us to continue to build his Kingdom of love here and now. There is also an accompanying guidebook to this text if you want to explore the ideas presented here through activities and additional reading designed to take you deeper into this discussion and into personal ownership and development of your philosophy and worldview.

FINAL EXHORTATION

I ask you to remember a few things as you read this book. First, this is not a traditional book on philosophy or apologetics. Professionals in those fields have already provided excellent resources on those topics. I am a husband, father, brother, son, friend, and fellow pilgrim who is offering a practical and useful way to organize the information, questions, and answers we are bombarded with on this adventure of life. In many respects, I am offering it to you because it works for me in my day-to-day endeavors to love and, as Ulysses says in Tennyson's poem, "drink life to the lees."[6] This book will not be able to prove the truth to you in the traditional sense of the word *prove*. It is not intended to do so. It is designed as a mirror for discovering your own object of trust and as a map for you to use as you continue your journey and quest for truth.

Second, I did not write this book to make you or anyone more "religious." I hope to show you truths that can break down walls, open locked doors, expose lies or fears, and invite you into joy, freedom, and love. I invite you to go beyond religion, trust lists, and worldviews into a relationship with *the* living, loving Being. The apostle John wrote of him, "You will know the truth, and the truth will set you free" (John 8:32). My unashamed, unambiguous, and ultimate hope is that this book brings you closer to the Christ, who can and will powerfully transform your life.

PART ONE

Trust and the Nature of Reality

CHAPTER 1

Created to Trust

Everyone trusts. The only way humans live, eat, sleep, move, communicate, and eke out an existence is to make decisions based on whatever we consider trustworthy. This has been the case throughout all of history. Even through seismic cultural shifts, the defining and redefining of races and religions, and the rising and falling of empires, people have made decisions based on whom or what they trust as really real, as worthy of trust. But also all through history, humans have differed on the object of this trust. They have not agreed on where to put their confidence. Both of these are still true today. We still operate on trust, and we humans do not agree on whom or what is worthy of that trust.

We give authority to whom and what we trust, and the more we trust something or someone, the more authority we give.

Who do you turn to when you have a complex decision to navigate? Many people turn to their parents, teachers, coaches, or mentors. Some people would never turn to a teacher or parent and do not have coaches or mentors. Many teachers are transformative; some are unfit. Many coaches are inspiring; some are simply abusive. Many mentors are true leaders; some are blind guides. We take medicine from doctors we trust; we steer clear of those who have poor reputations. I would not let a surgeon cut me open or an anesthesiologist put me under if I did not trust him or her with my life. We do not take our cars to mechanics we do not trust. I only rock climb with trusted friends. Friends we trust sway what we wear, eat, say, and watch. Pastors positively and negatively shape our lives and habits. The books you read and the movies you watch shape your daily activities and verbiage. The list goes on and on.

Consciously and subconsciously, whatever we give authority to or have given authority to in the past directly and indirectly influences our current thoughts and behaviors. Ultimately, and without being fully consciously aware of it, we each develop personal "lists" of what we deem to be worthy of our trust. These personal trust lists become the primary influence on how we view and interact with the world.

Unfortunately, not everything to which we give authority is worthy of our trust. Moreover, we often find ourselves in situations in which others assert their authority over us even though we do not trust them. This type of authority often uses fear, inflicts pain, devises external motivators, and exploits ignorance to influence behavior. It often takes great courage to address the issues of trust and trustworthiness, particularly when it involves changing what we put our trust in or finding freedom from unhealthy, unwanted situations of imposed authority. Many of these negative untrustworthy situations can be redemptively helpful in guiding us toward that which is truly trustworthy and life-giving. Additionally, these people and institutions can help us learn what not to do and who not to emulate—and why!

This is a great place to start our story. My hope is that this book leads you into a story of courage and freedom. Facing the truth about trust and authority, and potentially changing the motivation or object of our trust, could be the most courageous thing any of us will ever do. For some of us, standing firm in what we trust to be the truth in the face of opposition will take similar courage. This is where the adventure begins and, ironically, ends: in trust and courage.

CHAPTER 2

Faith and Faith Island

Trust is the norm. It is the only option we have to figure out the truth about our existence. Since absolutely nothing is 100 percent verifiable by anybody—not by a scientist, not by a guru—by necessity we all walk this truth journey by faith.

We all trust our eyes and brains, equipment and textbooks, theories and methods, predecessors and professors, scientists and doctors, parents and friends, teachers and preachers. Sometimes these people and tools prove to be unfaithful, and we lose trust, and faith and even hearts are broken.

However, the bits of information we deem trustworthy we tend to call *knowledge*. When we find something perpetually trustworthy, we use terms like *fact, proof,* or *logical truth*.

Many people have long desired to put an end to faith. They hope a staunch devotion to logic and reason can replace the need for faith and beliefs, which they say do not have "proofs" to support them. Writer G. K. Chesterton points out the fallacy of this idea: "It is idle to talk always of the alternative of reason and faith. Reason is itself a matter of faith. It is an act of faith to assert that our thoughts have any relation to reality at all."[1]

To put it bluntly: every worldview is based on faith, even ones that deny faith completely. This is an accurate and freeing statement, but it is not always easy for us to accept. It is hard for us to leave behind our blind confidence in "proofs" and the idea that we can know things with 100 percent certitude.

I want you now to imagine an island where everything in life is overtly based on faith. Every day, in every moment, all the people on the island live in acute, awake awareness that they have a perpetually faith-filled, moment-by-moment existence.

Imagine you were on a ship that wrecks near this island. You have taken refuge on the island and are able to observe its inhabitants closely. The natives wake up and have to *believe* they are getting out of their beds and then *believe* the eggs they are eating are real. They must have faith that their parents are really their parents, that the coffee is not poisoned, and that the tools they need to do their jobs will work. They must *believe* that the sun is actually warming them and that night will come in a few hours. You observe that these people live by faith all day, every day.

As you imagine this scenario, you might be confused or frustrated. You might be smirking because the point of the story has clicked. Maybe you're thinking, *That would be insane! How could anybody live?* Or maybe you have caught on and are wondering, *Isn't that how we all live every day?* In discussions when I raise this thought experiment, I often get a retort such as "No way! I don't have to believe I ate my eggs this morning; I just ate them!" Like it or not, believe it or not, the truth is that you are living on Faith Island right now, right where you are. The entire earth could be titled "Faith Island."

In my high school classes we discuss this idea until it clicks for everybody in the room. Often I will offer an A+ for the entire class if someone can give me just one thing they can prove and perfectly verify with 100 percent certitude. Take a moment and try to think of something right now. The painful turning point for the deepest skeptics comes when we collectively land on the conclusion that we all are very literally trusting our fallible eyes, hands, ears, tongues, noses, and ultimately our often malleable and fragile brains to make sense of the world. And admittedly, all of these perception tools have been inaccurate at some point and could be wrong at this very moment.

At this point, not surprisingly, it is fairly short work to comprehend that all of life, for all people, all the time is interpreted through the lens of trust and faith. Movies like *The Truman Show*, *The Matrix*, and *Inception* can be helpful here. Movies like these stretch our connections with what we trust, open our awareness, and help us engage with our immediate surroundings in profound ways. For example, *Inception* builds its plot on the main premise of this text: we trust thoughts and ideas. In the movie, characters are able to enter other people's dreams and subconscious thoughts and ultimately steal or "incept" core memories, thoughts, and ideas. During the key setup moment of the movie, the main characters are talking about incepting (planting and replacing) an idea in another character's mind. The protagonist quips, "The seed that we plant in this man's mind will grow into an idea. This idea will define him. It may come to change, well, it may come to change everything about him."[2] The underlying assumption is that we trust thoughts and ideas.

Movies like *Inception* can also help us evaluate the thoughts and ideas we trust and why. In another scene, the main group of inceptors are practicing "dream building." Right before their eyes and the eyes of the audience, one of the inceptors bends the city in half like a taco until it looks like an M. C. Escher painting. When we reach this scene, we instinctively know that the characters are in a dream—a city can't fold in half! Yet if we probe a little further, we realize that this is probably what the disciples felt like when they were in the boat and saw Jesus walking on the water, or when he fed five thousand people with one lunch, or when he calmed a raging storm with words, or when he told a dead girl to wake up and she did. They must have felt like they were in someone's dream—things like these don't usually happen! So why do we know the folding city is a dream and trust Jesus' miracles? I am not trying to elaborate on the trustworthiness of the Bible at this point—I trust that these things *did* happen. But that is the point: my belief in these events is based on what I *trust*. Movies like *Inception* can stretch us as viewers into examining or reexamining what we trust or do not trust and why. (More on the why later in this text.)

From me to you to every doctor, mathematician, religious leader, guru, and hard-core skeptic, everybody exists on Faith Island because faith (trust) is the only option for us every day that we live on this whirling, blue-and-green ball. And what we trust is embedded deep in our hearts and minds and directly affects how we interact with the world around us on a daily basis. It affects our reactions to the movies we watch, the stories we read and listen to, and the sacred texts we say we believe.

This idea may be shocking, but keep in mind that a life based on trust is not a bad thing. Despite the cynicism and brokenness in our world, much is worthy of our trust, and a healthy knowledge and understanding of whom and what we trust can give us an honest sense of security and confidence. I call these people and things that we choose to trust our personal "trust list," and we all use our trust lists to help us make the most of our grand existence and daily adventures, both individually and collectively. My trust list includes (but is not limited to) my imagination, my wife, the Bible, and my friends. I suspect that Richard Dawkins (a famous atheist) trusts science, genetic theories, several of his Oxford friends and scholars, atheist texts, and his own brain. Viewing the world as Faith Island is such a freeing way to approach our relationships with friends and teachers, professors and pastors, and people of other religions or even of no religion. It is a healthy approach to all our interactions anywhere on this planet. Everybody has a trust list because everybody is trusting something. Thus, this is a safe, engaging, honest, and conversational way to relate to each other that invokes dialogue and ownership.

Remember, one essential key for each person to accept at some point on this trust journey (the sooner the better) is that even the objective absolutes that many of us trust cannot be verified with 100 percent certitude. This is convenient for us to point out to people we disagree with, but it is also an inconvenient truth for us when that sentiment comes back in our direction. For example, I believe that God and God's Word are 100 percent trustworthy—yet I must admit that my access to God and God's Word are through that which is subjective and suspect: my brain, my emotions, my eyes, my ears . . . *myself.* I do believe absolute objective truth exists; I also believe that my personal access to that truth is subjective. Fortunately, when I read the Bible, I read that Jesus does not say that if you can prove you are right in a debate, you will be saved. He says that anyone who *believes* (that is, *trusts*) in him will be saved (see John 3:16).

Considering worldview through the lens of trust is a safe, healthy, life-giving, honest, and engaging way to interact with professors, bosses, and others in your community. It is empowering and honoring. *Everybody* is professing a trust list. Consequently, in my classes, I teach my students that they cannot (and should not) try to literally prove to others that there is a God. I can't prove that Jesus is the fullness of reality or that Jesus was and is God. I don't want to try to prove it. I confidently trust it; I wholeheartedly believe it. And if you believe it as well, you must have some sort of trust in the things that help you have buoyancy in these beliefs. If you don't believe Jesus was actually a real human being and also God in the flesh, it is simply and fundamentally because you are trusting other people and things than I am. Right here is where, if we were sharing some time and space together, we could enjoy the freedom of a kind conversation about what we each trust and why.

Personal trust lists are engaged the moment you wake up each day. Whatever you did when you woke up this morning, when you wake up every morning, I can guarantee that it involved your personal trust list. Maybe you read a few pages or lines from a sacred text, watched a TED Talk, scrolled through the news feed of your preference, listened to a podcast, meditated, connected with a friend or mentor, exercised, cranked a playlist, or simply chose not to feed your thoughts or heart with something external and pondered the day on your own.

At this point it might be fruitful to write down who and what is on your personal trust list. Who are the people you have given authority to in your life? Whose voices are you listening to? What beliefs or ideas govern your daily life? You may even want to take the next step of examining and contemplating the natural and even supernatural consequences of whom and what you trust.

What follows is space for you to write down who and what are on your current trust list. After you fill this out, I encourage you to take time to ponder the reflection questions. After you've thought these through, I suggest having a conversation with someone (preferably someone you trust) about these ideas.

MY CURRENT TRUST LIST
Date:
Location:

+ I trust

+ I trust

+ I trust

+ I trust

+ I trust

+ I trust

+ I trust

+ I trust

+ I trust

+ I trust

+ I trust

+ I trust

Additional thoughts:

REFLECTION QUESTIONS

1. Who or what is on your personal trust list? What do you tend to find trustworthy?
2. What makes someone or something trustworthy?
3. As you contemplate your trust list, why do you trust these things? On what basis are they worthy of your trust?
4. What should be on your trust list that is not?
5. Is there anything on your trust list that should be removed?
6. Do you think *you* are on anyone's trust list? Why or why not?

Trust Lists:
The Concept and the Tool

Not only is your worldview your view of the world, but it's your view for
the world. . . . You may not live what you profess, but you will live what
you believe. It's inescapable. We are great at professing things, but the
way we live really demonstrates what's at the root of what we believe.
[Our] worldview is not just a mindset; it is a will set. It's how we live our
lives, how we choose our priorities, and how we adopt preferences. . . .
You can determine a person's worldview just by asking the ultimate
questions, which deal with origin, meaning, morality, and destiny. . . .
The answers to these questions touch every single molecule of the
universe. . . . The answers affect you. . . . There are answers.

WILLIAM E. BROWN

Now that you've written and thought about your own trust list,
we're moving from personal trust lists to collective trust lists,
and we will look specifically at the trust lists of the four worldviews: idealism, materialism, monism, and theism. From a
philosophical and even a theological perspective, the trust lists
of these worldviews reveal the foundations of their perspectives on reality and their interactions with it. These worldview

trust lists form our core beliefs by providing authentic answers to some of the biggest questions of life. These answers also provide the substance of our shared isms, religions, and ways, and they are closely linked to our personal trust lists. Even when people are unaware of this connection, the daily, continual decisions that people make can be traced not only to their personal trust lists but to one of or a combination of the worldview trust lists.

As we develop our personal trust lists, we pull from these four lists. Unfortunately, many people are unaware of this. They haven't identified their own trust lists, nor have they recognized the consequences of trusting the four lists to answer the big questions they have.

Additionally, we often do not realize how much we are influenced by the personal trust lists of those around us. Their actions, choices, and conversations are also based on what they, individually, have chosen to trust, so as we observe and interact with them, our personal trust lists are affected by theirs, just as theirs, too, are influenced by those around them. As people form themselves into groups, their actions, choices, and conversations extend into the broader culture and shape cultural identity. Many people are unaware of how profoundly they and others are swayed by the broader macro cultures of which they are a part, and this lack of awareness leads to miscommunication, misunderstanding, friction, and tension in our homes and in local and global communities like churches, schools, neighborhoods, cities, and even countries.

There are great advantages in identifying our own personal trust lists and, on a larger scale, the lists of those with whom we share community. Furthermore, increased consciousness of where we place our trust develops both self-awareness and shared awareness. Consequently, the more we know about ourselves and others' trust lists, the more we are able to engage in healthy dialogue and shared understanding with others. As an example of how our personal trust lists are shaped by those around us, let's consider a question my daughter Anna asked when she was five years old. Our beloved yellow lab, Pup, had died, and Anna said, "Papa, where did Pup go?" Though she was asking specifically about our dog, she was also indirectly asking what will happen when she dies, when grandpa dies, when her papa dies. It was and is a universal question. Like Prince Hamlet, we all must ponder "the undiscovered country, from whose bourn no traveler returns,"[1] and this forces us to deal with the potential options of what actually happens after we die. How we answer that question directly affects the ways we approach daily life. Therefore, Anna's question was an important one, and my answer was also very important since she trusts me and has given massive authority to what I think. My answer would influence how she frames the weighty issues of life and death in her unfolding individual story and as a growing member of our immediate community. In many respects our questions and the various answers we all choose to trust are what directly create much of the dramatic tension in this unfolding global story we are all part of writing.

The issue at stake is there are different answers to Anna's question that have very different consequences, and the trust lists of the four major worldviews enable us to navigate this important scenario and others like it. For example, if I were to approach Anna's question as an idealist, I would tell her that Pup's physical suffering is over and the perfected components of Pup's spirit have been united with the ideal, one, eternal state of spiritual perfection that exists beyond the broken, lifeless, material body on the floor. Pup has ceased to exist, but glimpses and moments of the joy, love, and beauty we saw in Pup's snuggles, wags, licks, and walks will live on because they had their source in the spiritual, eternal ideals of goodness, truth, and beauty that exist beyond this finite world filled with death, pain, and decay. As Anna continues to grow with that in mind, she might seek solidarity on her journey in connection with the stories and themes found in Buddhism, much of Hinduism, and other religions or ways that pull from idealism.

On the other hand, if I were to approach Anna's question as an authentic materialist, I would tell Anna that Pup lived her life as well as she could, and it is now done because her broken body does not have the ability to continually conduct the electrical impulses needed for reacting to her environment. I would carefully explain that anything we call "alive" has this end. We were fortunate to be a part of Pup's existence, as she was to be part of ours. Pup's well-lived life full of joy, love, and adventure is now done, and we will dispose of her body before it starts to decay, just as we recycle or dispose of a broken electronic toy that cannot be fixed. As Anna grows, she might look for support to navigate the nuances of life and death in atheistic, nihilistic, and existential authors such as Friedrich Nietzsche, Jean-Paul Sartre, Albert Camus, Richard Dawkins, and Christopher Hitchens.

Alternatively, I could play the opening scene of Disney's *The Lion King* for Anna and approach this hard but hopeful aspect of Pup's journey like a complete monist. I would tell Anna that life and death are natural parts of existing in the universe. Pup is simply participating in the grand unfolding of the process of life and transformation that all existence goes through. The energy of life flows in and out of all living things, and Pup is connected to this life force. Her body was born and grew and lived and recently started the process of transformation into another form of existence through decay and dissolution. It is the unfolding, exciting adventure of participating in existence and transformation—like a little caterpillar that grows and wraps itself in a cocoon, turns into a butterfly, but then nourishes a bird, and on and on. Some call this the circle of life. It will happen to all of us and has been happening forever. If she trusts this to be true, Anna might look to Taoism and theosophy or possibly identify with the perspectives in the New Age movement.

Finally, I could talk about how God is a powerful, creative being who brought animals and humans into being. I could tell her one of the many creation stories like the influential one about Adam and Eve and all the animals in a loving, perfect relationship with their Creator and with each other. This would give some context for then talking with Anna about how this creative God has power over life and death and eternal life for all of creation. I could help her understand that I do not know exactly what has happened to Pup because none of us is God. Though God has revealed his nature to be loving, life-giving, and relational, God has not been specific about what happens to animals when they die. Therefore, God has intentionally put us in a position to trust him as the powerful, loving Creator with regard to what will happen to Pup now that her body has suffered the consequences of being a participant in the unfolding drama of our existence. I could talk to Anna about God's eternal Kingdom, where there is no longer any death. As she grows, Anna might gravitate toward the theistic religions, their leaders, and their texts to make sense of the complexities of life and death.

These are four very different answers with vastly different consequences and potentially polarizing outcomes. This situation highlights the important truth that the big questions in life—which occur daily and naturally all around us and sometimes come from five-year-old children—force us to use what we trust to develop responses. This scenario shows how this moment could powerfully influence the direction Anna takes as she continues her journey of choosing what she believes. I know, of course, that my response might not have much influence at all, but the point is that it could.

A foundational philosophical principle emerges at this point of our journey. Trust activates truth. When you or I or Anna trusts an idea, story, or principle, that which is trusted gains more and more authority in our daily decisions and potentially our whole lives. I remember the first time I leaned back on a rappel rope. There was a very specific moment where I was standing in my own power on the edge of the cliff, and then in a moment I made a shift of weight and trust, where I activated the power of the harness, rappel device, and rope to completely hold me. When the trustworthy gear was fully trusted, I was able to lean over the edge of the cliff. My first moment of rappelling launched me on a lifelong climbing journey in which I went from suspicion, to general trust, to activating my trust, to confident trust, to eventually becoming a rappel instructor helping others to trust. Again, trust activates truth.

When Anna was faced with Pup's death, she accessed the

perspective of someone she trusted. She willingly gave me authority in her life to help her make sense of the lifeless body of her furry friend, and I used what I trusted to craft the best response for her in that moment. As a philosophy teacher, I had many options to pull from to help her shape her perspective of reality and develop her own trust list and personal understanding of the story of her life. I want you to have these tools as you develop your own trust list.

CHAPTER 4

The Suicide of Thought

Let's review for a minute. First, everyone trusts, though we differ on whom or what we trust. Second, our daily lives are shaped by our personal trust lists. And third, our trust lists are greatly influenced by others' trust lists, including the trust lists of our communities.

But what if someone says none of that is true? What if someone claims there is no point to trusting, there is no real reality or validity? What if this person calls you foolish for trying to figure anything out?

In 1908, the seemingly prophetic G. K. Chesterton wrote, "There is a thought that stops thought. That is the only thought that ought to be stopped."[1] Chesterton is referring to a completely opposite way of life than that adopted by the fully thinking inhabitants of Faith Island. Chesterton aptly called this opposite way the "suicide of thought."[2] The internal monologue of someone slipping into the vortex of the suicide of thought goes something like this: *Since everything is based on trust and I have no means to verify anything, I cannot be 100 percent certain of anything. Therefore, I should not even try to figure out reality. And those who do try are wasting their time because they will never be certain, nor can they convince me of the certitude of anything asserted by either of us. Beyond lack of certitude lies the abyss of unverifiability.*

This is a classic agnostic thought process and the thought process of anybody who would like to wallow in the melancholic, half-hearted depression of latent postmodernism. In the mid to late 1900s, during the rise of powerful human ingenuity, prolific human industry, and potent humanistic philosophy, the influential thinkers of postmodernism expressed skepticism about life and existence, particularly about the self-absorbed humanism and overconfidence of industrial modernity in the early part of the twentieth century. Humans were displaying great power in creating, developing, and expanding our world while simultaneously and inversely powerfully destroying themselves, each other, and our world, particularly during the two world wars. Naturally and understandably, these thinkers freely questioned the validity of everything, including human thought itself. This inevitably led to questioning even the validity of human existence and forced a philosophical debate on the substance and nature of thought itself. It is easy to forget that the postmoderns were and are simply recapitulating the idea of Chesterton's "silly strips,"[3] the idea that we can deconstruct the nature and fabric of reality. The postmoderns remind us that we all have scissors and seam rippers, and we have the ability to dissect our interpretations of reality far beyond strips, down to minute pieces of thoughts and truths that we cling to as real and trustworthy—and then we can disassemble those as well.

Postmodern philosophers assert that our understanding of reality has been pieced together the way my son Elijah pieces together a village of LEGO bricks. And just as he does with his LEGO village, we can take apart the whole thing brick by brick and throw the pieces into a bucket. Then we have the ability to reconstruct a whole new village from the same pieces.

We easily forget that, on some level, we actually do live in an existential reality, a reality in which we have *chosen* to construct our personal view of the world from the individual thoughts we have *chosen* to put on our personal trust lists, from what we have *chosen* as trustworthy. This is what the entire concept of the trust list is built upon. Existentialism and deconstructive postmodern thinking explain how we all create our own version of little-*r* reality.

I find it helpful, with this in mind, to pause and sincerely honor the deconstructionists and even thank them for clarifying this foundational truth. It is appropriate to give them a high five or a fist bump. Then, after a long, quiet, awkward pause, quite frankly we need to get on with reconstruction and, more important, with living. Chesterton urges, "We have no more questions left to ask. We have looked for questions in the darkest corners and on the wildest peaks. We have found all the questions that can be found. It is time we gave up looking for questions and began looking for answers."[4]

The positive, encouraging truth gleaned from postmodern and existential thinking is this: when a powerful voice calls you to renew your mind or change the way you think, it is not only possible; it is a viable option. John the Baptist's voice still echoes from the wilderness and bounces off the cliffs of history two thousand years after he shouted, "Repent!" (which literally means "change your mind") to an entire nation of people. John spent his life calling people to change their minds, their worldviews, and their personal trust lists. If this change were not achievable, he would have been insane. But it *is* possible, and postmodern thinking gives us a glimpse into *why* it is possible for people to truly change what they believe and the way they perceive reality. Why is it possible? Because *we have real choice.* Furthermore, because there are at least these four basic perspectives on what is really real, these real choices have real, weighty consequences.

That being said, however, the suicide of thought can make the idea and process of building a trust list seem vain, arbitrary, and capricious. Postmodern thinking in the late 1900s began to blend with an existential philosophy that encouraged humans to focus *only* on one's personal, unique, individual, and thus irrefutable interpretation of reality. This has convinced many people to believe there is no Prime Reality, only fabricated, individual, unverifiable, subjective versions of reality. Whether intentionally or unintentionally, these existential, postmodern thinkers have spread a lie: since nothing is 100 percent trustworthy, it is therefore not worth trusting anything at all. When people are persuaded to believe there is no Prime Reality—no objective truth—they unwittingly embrace this lie.

Fortunately and unfortunately, the fact is that part of this lie is actually true: *nothing is 100 percent verifiable!* People are often distracted from the important difference between "verifiable" and "trustworthy," and thus, the suicide of thought is a formidable black hole that still has great gravitational force in our culture.

I know many loved ones who have slid into this terrifying, dark, lonely abyss. Some have done so willingly, some unwillingly. The crux of this chapter is this: if you or I believe we have found something absolutely trustworthy, in order to maintain any thoughtful dignity and integrity, we have to admit that our direct access to this "absolutely trustworthy" bit of information is through that which is not 100 percent trustworthy (our mind and our senses). Therefore, we are left with the formidable task of figuring out what is worth putting our trust in and then making the most of our delicate situation.

Richard Rohr comments on this task in *Creating Christian Community*:

> Much of Western culture is saddled with the conviction that humans must rationally create and explain all meaning for themselves. But this task is impossible, and so the search for meaning inevitably collapses into nihilism. The seeker gives up, assuming, "Since I can't figure it out, everything must be absurd and meaningless. There is no meaning, except what I manufacture, what I decide to believe." No civilization or community can be founded on this individualistic worldview because it is simply a collection of competing egos fighting for their dominant story based on private individuals' experience, hurts, perception, and education. This is most of North America and Europe today.[5]

Rohr accurately states that the suicide of thought cannot support civilizations and communities. It can even destroy them, and it can also destroy individuals. The hard, dark truth is that the suicide of thought often leads to the suicide of will and, sometimes, body. Fortunately—and this is more fortunate than we often realize—the truth that our entire interpretation of reality is based on trust equalizes the playing field for all of us. In every household and culture, we are truly like the inhabitants of Faith Island, each one of us living entirely by faith. Because nobody has the corner on the market or the ability to perfectly substantiate his or her understanding of the truth, we all have an opportunity to engage in healthy, open dialogue. This can foster compassionate community marked by honor and dignity, but this is only possible if we are humble enough to be honest about our inability to completely, objectively verify our own trust lists when we are in conversation with those who are trying to change their trust lists or with those who are struggling to find something or someone who is trustworthy.

I have found that the only way out of the vortex of the suicide of thought is to actually make a real choice. In the first half of Chesterton's chapter "The Suicide of Thought" (in his book *Orthodoxy*), he takes his reader into what the suicide of thought is. Fortunately, for the rest of the chapter, he helps the reader see how to get out of it. This is a complex matter, philosophically speaking, but here we go. If we make real choices, then we do actually trust something. The natural result of making a choice for something means something is trusted and other choices and things are excluded. For example, if someone chooses to be a vegetarian, he or she will naturally exclude meat from meals. If I choose to wear my running shoes, I exclude my sandals. If my friend as a theist chooses to trust in Allah and the Koran to explain his existence, then he naturally excludes the primary tenets of atheistic materialism. Choice is the essence and life-blood of trust.

If you and I walk out our doors, eat, talk, interact with humans, and live a life (even a meager one), we have a trust list because we will be making choices. And when we are making choices, we are exerting trust in what we are choosing. When we choose, we are excluding. In doing so, we place ourselves somewhere on the grid of these four philosophies with their trust lists. We place ourselves somewhere in their various stories. This is why it can be helpful to see life as a journey of discovery. And, yes, as we travel this journey, we may find something untrustworthy and need to make different choices based on our experiences.

This journey of discovery requires us to keep thinking, keep trusting, keep living, and keep finding what is trustworthy. If we keep the fire lit under the kettle of our thinking, our aware-ness will boil our thoughts down to meet the reality in which we find ourselves.

We can despair in the midst of this journey or make the most of it. One of my students insightfully pointed out we can also distract ourselves or be distracted from building an effective, functional trust list. My preference, of course, is that you consider this journey as an adventure, but whatever your response, at the very least, don't lie to yourself through con-structing a false sense of certitude in your facts, knowledge, or proofs. All of life is based on trust, and we are all on Faith Island together. We must remember this as we mindfully create knowl-edge and facts and proofs out of that which is trustworthy. We are always trusting these bits of information.

And here is where the suicide of thought mutates into generative hope. The book of Proverbs says, "Hope deferred makes the heart sick, but a dream fulfilled is a tree of life" (Proverbs 13:12). This proverb is not about not getting what we want; it is about ceasing to hope at all. So here is a bit of life-giving hope in a potentially arid and dry chapter at the beginning of this book: *The suicide of thought does not actually exist.*

I am glad you kept reading. It is a paradoxical truth. If the suicide of thought kills our ability to think, positioning us to stop trusting anything, including our own thoughts, the only way we landed in this suicide of thought is by trusting the thought that our thoughts are not trustworthy.

If you are trusting your thought that your thoughts are not trustworthy, you *are* trusting something—you are trusting that thought. Therefore, it is no longer the suicide of thought. If you can trust the thought that your thoughts are not trustworthy, then you can trust other thoughts too. The key here is it is a matter of choice. We choose which thoughts to trust based on their effects on our minds, bodies, and souls. Which thoughts will you choose to trust on your journey?

This truth is at the bedrock of all existence. We trust thoughts. If you can make a real choice, then this is the time to start choosing which thoughts you are going to trust. This is the adventure of life; this is the marrow and the impetus and the traction of life.

This chapter ends with a double irony. If we as humans cannot make real choices, then we cannot go into the suicide of thought, and, ironically and terrifyingly, we cannot get out of it. Without choice, there is no autonomy and no real self-direction. There is no real *self*; there is only an illusory perception of self in which there actually is no self. There is only what one might call *awareness*.

Truth be told, without free will there is no chance for real love or authentic relationship, and these, I would claim, are the foundation of meaning for human existence. C. S. Lewis, a man who pushed atheism to its intellectual limits, notes this tension and potential in *Mere Christianity*.

He states:

> God created things which had free will. That means creatures which can go either wrong or right. Some people think they can imagine a creature which was free but had no possibility of going wrong; I cannot. If a thing is free to be good it is also free to be bad. And free will is what has made evil possible. Why, then, did God give them free will? Because free will, though it makes evil possible, is also the only thing that makes possible any love or goodness or joy worth having. A world of automata—of creatures that worked like machines—would hardly be worth creating. The happiness which God designs for His higher creatures is the happiness of being freely, voluntarily united to Him and to each other in an ecstasy of love and delight compared with which the most rapturous love between a man and a woman on this earth is mere milk and water. And for that they must be free.[6]

Thus, choice and trust are the essence of all meaningful existence. Without these key ingredients, there may be life, but as has been seen here and as will be further developed later in this book, an understanding of life without choice and trust has potent consequences. Inversely, the awareness of choice and trust creates an avenue for autonomy and self-direction. It creates an understanding of and motivation for an empowered, engaged, and meaningful life.

CHAPTER 5

What Is Really Real?

As I mentioned in the introduction, my approach to worldview, and thus philosophy, is simple and practical. It builds on and extends the iconic works on the nature and outcomes of our beliefs about Prime Reality generated by Socrates, Plato, and Aristotle. In essence, these brilliant minds helped us clearly see that the spiritual (the nonmaterial) and the material are the two basic ingredients for the fabric of reality. Most philosophers agree that Plato's and Aristotle's works on the nature of Prime Reality are a foundation for all human interaction concerning reality.

Over thousands of years, humans have developed trust lists based on their perspectives of the spiritual world and the material world. As mentioned before, a logical grid built from these two entities results in four foundational trust lists: idealism, materialism, monism, and theism.

This is the tension of the big story we all find ourselves in on this planet. Generally speaking, there are four different story line options that help us make meaning out of our lives. The law of noncontradiction (which states that a thing cannot be true and not true at the same time) and the reality of personal experience create distinctions between these stories that seem insurmountable. As we've seen, we all live by faith, and no one has the corner on the market when it comes to verifying the truth of his or her story and trust list with 100 percent certitude. Every story and trust list seems to be true, at least to someone, yet we know intuitively and logically that all of the trust lists cannot be independently true at the same time.

My approach is not simply another shallow, slippery attempt to advocate relativism or universalism. Even though there are four basic attempts to understand what is really real, and from these four basic trust lists (or worldviews) there are hundreds of religions and isms, there is ultimately only one true Prime Reality—one real story line that is the unfolding of the true story of humanity. I have sometimes been accused of creating "straw men" in my approach to religion. But those who accuse me of this, despite generally being well-meaning, are missing one of the essential components to my approach to worldview: I am taking a *philosophical* approach, not a comparative religion approach, to understanding our connections with Prime Reality. My goal is to reveal and connect truth found in all worldviews. I am not combatively dismantling all religions except my own. I have worked with devout philosophers and religious leaders to build an honest, accurate representation of all four worldviews with dignity and honor. Although this approach to worldview is not focused on religion, it will set you up well for the next comparative religion class, book, or conversation that you encounter.

Every great adventure story is driven along by tension, and there is plenty of tension in this discussion. Thus, we have the main plot of our story.

THE TENSION OF THE FOUR PERSPECTIVES

We will call these four perspectives the main characters in this story. The setting is planet Earth, and the plot is the quest for truth. Each character is vying for the victory of being the most credible, the most trustworthy, and the most accurate worldview. Pure idealists trust that only the spiritual truly exists as ultimate, eternal, Prime Reality. Authentic materialists trust that reality consists exclusively of the measurable material world of the periodic table of elements, electricity, and waves. Complete monists (or pantheists) posit that both realms are real and exist as extensions of each other—although dual in nature, they are essentially one entity with no actual distinctions or real separation. Sincere religious theists believe both domains exist, but the spiritual realm and the material realm coexist independently, interdependently, and intradependently, with deep connectivity yet real distinctions.

These four perspectives contain and generate all the isms, religions, ways, beliefs, cults, heresies, ideologies, and worldviews that have ever been, and all seekers of truth everywhere believe in some variation of one of these perspectives. Therefore, every individual will, by necessity, find himself or herself somewhere on the grid of these four trust lists when answering life's essential queries and tensions. The thrust of this entire opening section is this point: our interpretation of reality and, in consequence, the quality of our lives are based on what we trust. Therefore, the question of trustworthiness—of what makes something or someone worthy of trust—is a great question. It might be the *greatest* question.

This question of trustworthiness has the ability to shift the paradigm of the global conversation on philosophy, theology, and worldview. If we acknowledge that our different beliefs share the same bedrock of trust, we can change the tone, nature, and direction of our discourse from diametrical opposition to dialectical conversation. We must work together to pursue what is ultimately worthy of all our trust, and we must be honest with each other in the process. We must not settle for any supposed "truth" that is not holistic, complete, loving, whole, unifying, and life-giving for people of all races, of both genders, of all ages, of all economic and societal statuses. We must, together, pursue a capital-*T* Truth that is worthy of being called Prime Reality, that unifies us, that is not simply one truth at the expense of all other truths but that can hold many differences together. This capital-*T* Truth cannot merely be true here or there but must be true everywhere. If it is going to be called a *world*view, it must be a view *of* the entire world, *for* the entire world, for all times, not just this one and not simply my personal view of the world.

We can then say that the trustworthy thing or person that most closely aligns with all these ideas of truth *is* Prime Reality, the true story of the universe. This is the standard by which we measure our personal trust lists and the trust lists of the four perspectives. For as long as we have lived, humans have claimed their personal and collective trust lists to be the truth—to be Prime Reality. You probably have the same idea about your personal trust list, as does the group to which you belong. In this book, I am challenging you to not only examine the trust lists of other worldviews but to examine yours as well, to measure it by the standards of Prime Reality.

In the next two parts of this book, I share the viewpoints of the four perspectives about some of life's greatest themes and the answers the four perspectives give to seven major life questions. I created these trust lists to provide you with a clear map for approaching and understanding the daunting array of worldviews and religions and also to help you understand and evaluate where you and others fall on this map. Remember, in our search for peace and authenticity, we are all trusting one (or perhaps a blended form) of the four answers. Again, a key to unlocking the potential of this approach is to keep in mind that I am not explaining the nuances and minutiae of all the religions and isms. This book is not designed to give you the "what" or the "how" of religions; it is specifically designed to offer you a glimpse at the "why" of all of the religions and isms. When applied correctly, this approach will not only enhance your understanding of why followers of other religions or isms do what they do; it will also help you know more of why *you* behave and think the way you do.

The lines between these four worldviews can get blurry as people seek to develop personal trust lists to navigate daily life. To help bring those lines into focus, I have added the distinctive adjectives *pure*, *authentic*, *complete*, and *religious* in front of the titles of the four views: idealism, materialism, monism, theism. These adjectives remind us that we rarely find people or religions that wholeheartedly adhere to only one of the four philosophical options. Hinduism, for example, has a unique blend of monism and idealism. Like idealists, their spiritual journey essentially consists of striving for perfection and union with god, yet once they achieve it, they realize that they themselves were actually what they were seeking all along. Buddhism split off from Hinduism for many reasons, but one was Hinduism's attachment to the material realm. Many atheists blend theism with atheistic principles, holding on to a form of free will and objectivity for morality that can only exist in theism (morality appeals to something outside of materialism, which complete materialists reject). Many theists live and act like materialists, rejecting supernatural activities like angels and miracles yet clinging to some form of a creator God. There are so many of these people that some pastors and writers have named this group the "unbelieving believers."

It's also worth mentioning at this point that every semester I get one or two students who ask why I only really address monotheism and not polytheism. The main reason is that in this text we are focusing on philosophy and not religion. We do not have the time or space to describe the detailed functions of religious practices and beliefs when others do so thoroughly elsewhere. Furthermore, most polytheistic religions of the past have been absorbed into mythology. When we apply the philosophical trust list approach to a detailed study of polytheism, we eventually land in two polytheism camps. One camp is philosophically and even theologically more like monotheism, and the other is not actually polytheism or even theism at all.

In the first camp of polytheistic religions that are actually polytheistic, with multiple individual gods and goddesses, there is always one god who is the prime mover, first in authority over all the lesser gods. This type of polytheism, when put under the light of philosophy, will point us to the top god as the main god when answering the big philosophy question of "who is God?"

The second camp is where Buddhism and Hinduism are often viewed as polytheistic because of their idols and statues. When taken seriously and put under the philosophical and religious microscope, these idols and statues and the gods they represent are not actually gods in the literal meaning of a "god"—a "divine autonomous being." They are merely representations or images of the one true spiritual "state of being." These gods are more like the colors a prism separates out from pure light, only pointing devotees beyond themselves into the pureness of the good, the beautiful, and the true, which exist beyond essence and being, especially beyond statues and idols. Nirvana does not have legs, arms, and a mind, nor does ultimate reality in Hinduism. That is why this text focuses primarily on monotheism when considering religious theism. Most polytheistic religions that are still professed today can be mapped onto the four worldviews described in this text.

As you read the following pages, if you fail to find yourself drawing from any of these four worldview lists, it usually indicates a lack of awareness of the object of your trust or of the natural consequences your choices create. Being unaware usually results in feeling overwhelmed, underwhelmed, unfulfilled, and unfruitful, or angry, bitter, and resentful.

Generally, appropriate alignment and awareness of the real consequences of our choices, especially those concerning the nature of reality, create unity, peace, and freedom while simultaneously reducing internal conflict and confusion. However, the opposite may, in fact, be true: an awareness of the "why"

behind what you believe could be quite painful and unnerv-
ing. Nevertheless, that pain is often the most effective path
toward freedom and healing. Consider this as the difference
between treating the symptoms of sickness and treating the
cause of sickness. An honest assessment of the object of trust
and the outcomes of this trust ultimately leads to clarity and
a deeper sense of ownership and vitality. Thus, this accessible
approach to worldviews can be empowering, engaging, freeing,
and inspiring.

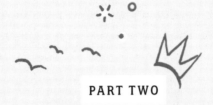

PART TWO

Philosophy and the Four Views of Reality

CHAPTER 6

Philosophy:
A Practical Tool

Philosophy... moulds and constructs the soul; it orders our
life, guides our conduct, shows us what we should do and
what we should leave undone; it sits at the helm and directs
our course as we waver amid uncertainties. Without it, no one
can live fearlessly or in peace of mind. Countless things that
happen every hour call for advice; and such advice is to be
sought in philosophy.

SENECA

In the last part we exposed the perils of not examining our own
beliefs, of not knowing our own trust lists, and we also juxta-
posed the optimism and hope that come from a clear, authentic,
life-giving trust list with the dangers of the suicide of thought.
Now it is time to move forward in the process of discovery
and examination. This is a wonderful process with rich results.
When we find that what we believe is *trustworthy* and then surrender to trust, we do not have to live either thoughtlessly or
in the suicide of thought, nor do we have to live in ignorance
of what others choose to believe and why they have potentially
made those choices. A healthy trust list has great power. It can
lead to a thoughtful, well-lived life and to meaningful, healthy
relationships with others.

G. K. Chesterton pursued just such a life. He thought through his trust list. He journeyed through life aware of his philosophy, he knew the "why" behind his beliefs, and he understood and accepted the reality of trust. Author Philip Yancey, who wrote the foreword to an edition of Chesterton's *Orthodoxy*, dubbed him the "prophet of mirth"[1] due to his ability to artfully engage others in sincere dialogue through wit, whimsy, and laughter. Because Chesterton knew and practiced all this, he was able to experience great gratitude for his life. This is revealed in his poem "Evening":

Here dies another day
During which I have had eyes, ears, hands
And the great world round me;
And with tomorrow begins another.
Why am I allowed two?[2]

Chesterton had a sense of joy-filled privilege for his day-to-day life, and he believed life is beautiful and purposeful. This is what I want for you, but I understand you may not feel the same as Chesterton. It's not always easy to see life as a privilege because it is often difficult to make sense of the world and the daily decisions we have to make. So how do we do this? How do we discover gratitude for life? How do we make sense of it?

We use the tool of practical philosophy. Practical—or applied—philosophy helps us see that we already have a framework in place that guides our decisions and helps us "make sense" of the world. Practical philosophy helps us honestly examine and understand this framework—our views—and better understand the views of others. Therefore, it allows us to engage in respectful dialogue and relationship with others, even those with very different views.

Practical philosophy is an important tool with vast amounts of power, so as with all powerful tools, some instruction and caution is needed before we actually begin using it. I inherited my grandfather's leather-handled antique hammer. It's clearly worn and broken in from frequent use. A hammer is *meant* to be used. It is not an object to be put on display in pristine condition or simply talked about or waved in the air. My Grandpa Sam, who loved to build, *used* his hammer. Philosophy is a tool like a hammer. If we are not using it to build and construct our trust lists and worldviews, it is as if we have bought a hammer simply to carry it around or display it. It will look, feel, and *be* ostentatious.

So philosophy, like a hammer, is meant for use. Here's another similarity. Though a hammer is a powerful, focused tool, almost anybody can learn to use one. My seven-year-old twins love pounding nails and building birdhouses or fairy gardens with hammers. Elijah, Anna's twin brother, is like my grandfather; he loves to use tools with purpose. Grandpa Sam was a master craftsman; Elijah is what we might call on his way to becoming a master. Another similarity is that a hammer can be useful for demolition and deconstruction as well as for building (see chapter 4). If I need to renew my mind and change my perspective, I can use philosophy as a hammer to carefully pull apart the nails and boards of what I previously trusted, in order to create space for an addition or a new kitchen—a shift in perspective. I could also use philosophy like a sledgehammer and swing it around for an extreme makeover, creating space for a whole new house—a new way to see the world and thus a new way to live in the world. Whether the tool of philosophy is used for big or small projects, it requires skill, and with skill the tool of philosophy can be creative or destructive.

Because philosophy is a tool, it has neutral moral value. Consider common items like a cell phone or a car. In and of themselves they are morally neutral—neither good nor evil. Therefore, as tools, their value, usefulness, and moral implications are determined by the intent and motivation of their users. A hammer can be used to build, renovate, or repair, but it can also be used to smash windows or even skulls. The tool of philosophy has sometimes been used in just this cruel way. Thus, we must be hypervigilant to use it in safe, honoring, loving, and generative ways. Furthermore, due to the powerful nature of the tool of philosophy, a lack of experience, awareness, character, or skill creates an implied danger—like the difference between giving my young son a traditional hammer and nail gun.

I find it intriguing and overwhelming to watch the latest Star Wars or superhero movies with worldview and philosophy in mind. I know that philosophy and worldview are powerful tools. And when I watch these movies, I notice that both the heroes and the villains are powerful individuals endowed with superpowers that make them each unique. What is most striking is that the core difference is found in their character—the heroes are loving, generous, and kind. The best villains are noticeably complex and relatable yet ultimately selfish, cruel, and destructive. The superpowers could almost always be considered neutral tools; it is how each individual character uses their powers that makes them a hero or a villain. If this book empowers you—in the literal sense of the word, "to give more power to"—with the superpowers of philosophy and answers to the big questions of life yet does not help or inspire you to become more kind, honoring, and loving in the process, it could be helping to create more villains instead of heroes. This is the risk of education, a huge but necessary risk. When we are not careful in how we use philosophy, not only does it damage those around us; it damages us. When we use philosophy with pretense, we become foolish. When we use it with ill intent, we become cruel. There has been and is too much abuse and cruelty caused by misuse of philosophy, as well as by the misuse of theology, doctrine, and religion. When any of these tools are abused and misused, they become toxic and destructive; they spread fear and confusion; they poison everything.

But the opposite is also true: when philosophy is used well, it is a powerful instrument for good. It leads to good thought and to good action. Margaret Mead is thought to have said, "Never doubt that a small group of thoughtful, committed citizens can change the world. Indeed, it is the only thing that ever has." We frequently see the slogan "Be the change you want to see in the world." And Anne Frank declared, "How wonderful it is that no one has to wait, but can start right now to gradually change the world!"[3] Improving your own perspective of the world is a great way to start improving the world itself.

We will use philosophy to improve our perspective of the world. First, we will use it to understand and examine the framework we already have in place—the framework that guides our decisions and helps us "make sense" of the world. We can think of this framework as a house, a house we live in every day, that shapes our lives—whether we realize it or not. The trust lists and their answers to life's big questions have framed our houses. One of the goals of this book is for you to see the shape of the house you are in and, using philosophy as a tool like a hammer, to either remodel it or rebuild it with a greater understanding of it. The house that you live in would be what some people call your religious beliefs, like the Anglican approach to Christianity, or your ism, like atheism or pantheism. Isms and religions give us the day-to-day framework and context for interacting with people and making daily decisions, particularly concerning morality and relationships. The first part of this book revealed that trust is the foundation of the house; it's what the house is built on. Trust is also the concrete and the beams, as well as the screws, the glue, the nails, and the brackets. Trust holds the house up and holds it together. Part 1 established the truth that all the different trust lists are made out of the same material: every house, no matter its ism or faith, is founded on and held together by trust. The stronger your trust and the more trust-worthy your materials, the stronger your house foundation and support system will be.

In part 2, we will move from the foundation up to the lumber and framework, to the plumbing and electrical work that is hidden behind the walls and paint. As we look at the big questions and the ways the four major trust lists answer them, we will see that natural and in many cases spiritual consequences are attached to the various worldviews, just as a home's style is determined by the decisions a home builder makes. By the end of this part, after we have examined all the different belief possibilities, all the different answers of the four trust lists, you should feel as if you are in a home decor showroom displaying all the options for making the house a place that feels like your home.

CHAPTER 7

The Power of a Question

[Conversation] is the most remarkable thing human beings do.

RICHARD SAUL WURMAN,
CREATOR AND FORMER CHAIR OF THE TED CONFERENCE

One of the best ways to improve our perspective on the world is through conversation—through sharing our big questions and answers with others and listening carefully to theirs. These conversations can change perspectives—and therefore the world—but these conversations are rare. Usually, people with very different trust lists avoid conversation about life's biggest questions, and often when they do attempt dialogue, they end up talking *around* each other, and the conversation is unproductive or even divisive. Authentic, transforming dialogue requires the participants to have some common understandings: they must be aware of their own trust lists, and they must also have awareness of and a willingness to listen to others' trust lists, even those radically different from their own.

These are the kinds of conversations I want you to be able

to have, and this is why we will be looking at how the four major perspectives answer life's biggest questions. We will look closely at their trust lists. My hope is that this will help you gain clarity on your own trust list and gain new hope, joy, peace, introspection, and momentum as you understand who or what you are trusting. As you do this, you will understand more fully the truths of Faith Island: we are *all* trusting something, and we trust in order to resolve the tensions we see in our world and in our personal lives. The consequences for trusting various options vary greatly, but the truth of Faith Island allows for a safe venue to explore the motivation, the "why" behind the beliefs we have. Eventually, these deep understandings can give us insight into and invite genuine acceptance of others and allow us to engage in meaningful, rich, and honoring discourse. And *these* are the kinds of conversations that can change our perspectives—and the world.

Before we move forward, however, we must first go back, back to the foundations of reality we discussed in chapter 5: that the material and the spiritual (the nonmaterial) are the two essential elements in the composition of reality. This is the view of Prime Reality from Socrates, Plato, and Aristotle. The four major worldviews are distinct from one another because of their perspectives on these two elements, which lead to very different conclusions about life. This is the foundational premise of my approach to worldview. Our interpretation of Prime Reality (what is really real) sets the tone for our entire trust lists. It all starts with what we perceive and trust to be really real. All the answers to every worldview question naturally unfold from here, making this approach to worldview memorable, manageable, and meaningful.

Here, again, are the four different perspectives:

+ **Pure idealism**, which views only the spiritual as really real
+ **Authentic materialism**, which trusts in only the measurable material realm
+ **Complete monism**, which accepts both the spiritual and the physical realms as fully real with complete unity and no authentic distinctions
+ **Religious theism**, which believes in the reality of both the spiritual and the material realms as deeply connected but with real distinctions

Next we must review *why* these four perspectives developed conclusions about the nature of reality. Each perspective is trying to answer the big questions that arise naturally from the details of everyday life, questions even young children all over the planet have already encountered. As they have dealt with the death of a beloved pet or simply as they've been told to share toys or food, they've bumped up against the mysteries of the universe. They begin asking, "Why, Papa?" and "Why, Mama?" soon after they begin to babble, and they will continue to do so. We are naturally inquisitive as a species, and as we tread the earth, soar through the stratosphere, and spiral into space (even if only in our imaginations), we wonder and ask questions—*big* questions.

In this book we will deal with seven of the big questions. While there are many more we must wrestle with individually and in community, these seven reflect questions all humans have asked, are asking, or will one day need to ask in order to help them understand themselves and the people and world surrounding them. The seven questions we deal with in this book—and all questions—are the natural response to what life throws at thoughtful, introspective, aware, autonomous beings. The big questions we will explore are similar to those James Sire posed in his influential book *The Universe Next Door*.[1] Although Sire did not originate the idea of the "big questions of life," he and many other philosophers made them colloquial, as they should be, and I tip my hat to them. I have reworked seven of the "big questions" for the focused purposes of this book and the trust lists. These seven are meant to be representative, not encompassing. I'm sure we could come up with twenty big questions or boil them down to fewer than seven. That is not the point. The point is that by practicing with these seven, we become familiar with the process of digging beneath the surface and looking at the trust inherent in every big question.

Dr. Charles Bressler was one of the most inspiring literary criticism professors I have had. While I was in college, he introduced me to the basic structure of the four worldviews and the big questions of philosophy. He trained his students to analyze and interpret literature written from each of the worldviews and also to read critically through the lens of the views. It was life transforming, and I owe him credit for planting the seeds of this trust tool. I also learned from him the value of a safe and honoring conversation space where we can ask and lean into any of life's hardest and most complex questions. That is what I strive to foster in my classroom and conversations; it is what I hope for my readers as well. I hope this text can loosen the tongues of those who want to become more comfortable with openly talking about those questions we too often shy away from—the big, hard life questions. We often shy away because we fear unsatisfying half-answers, and we dislike the answers available. We often shy away because life's big questions, when faced straight on, remind us again that all the answers are based on trust. This unsettles us, and we don't like feeling unsettled.

But avoidance does us no good—we will eventually have to answer, explicitly or implicitly, these questions or others like them. So let us move forward with courage. Let us explore the big questions and the ways we humans have answered them through a closer look at the four major worldviews. Let us pry open the door to our own views and the very different views of others. In doing so, let's create the type of understanding that will lead to further dialogue and further growth—because what we trust about reality has tremendous importance in our day-to-day routines as well as in the overarching story lines of our lives.

Let's begin by looking at the questions themselves.

1. What is the nature of reality? What is really real?

This is a great place to start all conversations concerning worldview. This is the root of all four options, and each option is distinct in the way it answers this question. Most of the questions that follow are, at their core, related to this one.

2. Who or what is God?

Everyone has to interact with this question. Most philosophers agree that our answers to this question shape our entire life and directly guide our responses to any other questions. A. W. Tozer famously quipped that your answer to this question is the most important thing about you. I wholeheartedly agree, for the religious and nonreligious alike. Depending on what we trust to be true, God may be just a word, a concept, a theory, a person, a spiritual being, oneself, the unnameable and unknowable, the Creator . . . God has meaning for almost everyone, even the most popular atheists, for they understand that even if they do not believe in God, they still have to directly interact with other people who do, and they still have to deal with the popular concept that infuses our global conversation. In a single class of just twenty-five students I can have individuals who believe God to be cruel, distant, immanent, within, selfish, egocentric, loving, generous, manipulative, uncaring, personal, abstract, disengaged, relational, abusive, dead, a joke, a lover, a friend, a teacher, a guide, a hoax . . . The twenty-five students I have in just one of the five classes I teach each day can have twenty-five different perspectives of God and thus twenty-five different approaches to their relationship with God, and thus their relationship with themselves and with those sitting next to them. What do you believe about God?

3. What is a human being? What is humankind? (Who am I? What am I?)

We all have asked or are asking, "Who am I?" and "What am I?" These are foundational questions that have profound implications, particularly in relation to the other questions listed here. Are we individuals? Are we distinct? Are we free beings, or are we a connected part of something or someone else . . . or both? Do we have nonmaterial souls, or are we simply sacks of chemicals? Are we puppets or self-directed or not directed at all?

4. What is the basis of and standard for morality? How do I decide between right and wrong, and who or what is the basis for moral authority?

This question asks whether morality is objectively real. If so, where did it come from, and why do we have to obey a particular moral code? This is why authority is a critical part of this question. Does a moral code have any real authority over me, and if so, why? If an ethical moral code does exist, can I change it? Why would I submit to an ethical moral code that I did not make? What is the difference between ethical moral codes and religious moral codes and social moral codes? Do I get to decide what is right or wrong, or does someone else?

5. What happens to humans at death?

Death permeates our world. What is death? Is death something to be feared or embraced? Is death an end or a beginning? Is it the beginning of a new real adventure or the continuation of this eternally unfolding adventure or the end of everyone's adventure? Does death offer hope, or does death end hope? Is death simply a concept? Can I define death however I choose, or is it defined for me?

6. What is the meaning and purpose of human history? What is the essence of human interaction and relationships?

These questions are not always included in lists such as this one, but I keep them as part of this tool because we all have memories, individually and collectively (as part of a family, a community, a nation, a people), and these memories profoundly affect us. This question helps us understand and define meaning for each day in the context of countless memories and eras of human history. When we seek answers to this question regarding history, we are drawn further into the mystery of origin—another big question. Deep thought about this question also gives perspective on the concept of story, a story with a beginning, middle, and possibly an end.

7. Why are we here? Where are we going? What is the purpose of human existence? What is the purpose of living for tomorrow?

Whether we realize it or not, we all spend a lot of time thinking about our purpose. We are enjoying or pursuing or denying or dreading or even despairing over it. Questions about purpose are often the most personal and powerful of all questions, and our answers set the tone and atmosphere not only for day-to-day living but also for our lives as a whole. Like a soundtrack for a movie, our understanding of our purpose is always present, providing a backdrop for the action of our lives, creating and sustaining the mood.

SEVEN QUESTIONS, FOUR PERSPECTIVES

Now we're ready to explore how the four perspectives answer these big questions. In this section, I want to give each worldview equal space and respect. Though earlier in this book I shared my personal worldview—that Jesus Christ is the fullness of reality—please understand it is not my intention to set up "straw men" in this section, nor in any part of the book. I do not want to present these worldviews—each of them held by many, many human beings—in a fallacious way that makes it easy to knock them down. In the past twenty years, I have had many students share with me that they are atheists, Buddhists, New Agers, or Muslims, and I tell them that if they pay careful attention to this philosophical approach to worldview, they should gain deeper insight and awareness into why they believe what they say they believe as well as into the extensive natural consequences of their particular trust list. If they choose to continue in their beliefs, this philosophical approach will also help them develop authenticity in these beliefs and in the practice of them.

Most of my teaching career has been in private Christian education, and nearly every year a brave student or two have sidled up to me at the beginning of the semester and covertly told me they are an atheist or a Buddhist (or a follower of something other than Christianity) and that they are excited to publicly and privately destroy yet another teacher who will try to manipulate or shame their beliefs. While this is supremely ironic for the Buddhist, I calmly assure these students it is not my desire to manipulate or bully them or anybody. If this is where you are, I would tell you that if you truly want to be an atheist (or Buddhist or anything else), you should pay close attention to this section because I can help you be a true, authentic, well-informed one. My goal is the goal of all loving philosophers and most loving parents and most seasoned administrators, regardless of their personal religion or trust list. It is to use philosophy to create a safe, honest setting for informed consent for one's beliefs. I want to provide you with the necessary tools, information, and clarity to seriously study your personal trust list and take ownership of it. (Of course, I would also encourage you to read part 3, about how Jesus

Christ is the fullness of reality and how each of the four world-views finds its completion in Christ.)

This book, then, is the result of a twenty-five-year journey of dialoguing with others about their worldviews. It is in many ways an intentional collaboration with people whose trust lists are very different from mine. I deeply desire that this book present each of the four major worldviews with honesty and honor, with the utmost integrity and dignity. Please be assured that many thought leaders, religious leaders, philosophers, and pilgrims from all faiths and perspectives have tested the authenticity of these lists.

On the practical front, I also want to make these views accessible, so I've chosen to present the answers in two formats. First, we will look at the information by the questions. In the next few pages, the seven questions are listed, followed by a short version of each perspective's answers. This kind of overview will allow you to easily compare and contrast the answers. In the second format, each perspective gets its own chapter, and its answers are more fully developed. This allows us to take a closer look at each view in isolation from the others.

As you read both the overview and the closer looks, I suggest you imagine you have just entered a big party and are being introduced to various people. Some of these people you know well already. You're happy to see them and feel comfortable connecting with them. You have a lot of common ground, so conversation flows smoothly. Some of your new acquaintances, though, are people you've only heard about (perhaps I told you about them for the first time in the past few chapters). You've never actually met them, but you've prejudged some of them, and you have a predisposition either for or against them. I know enough about human nature to realize that some of us are going to enter this party carrying baggage of hatred, condemnation, egocentric thinking, and alienation; some will enter the party with the desire to classify and delineate people with language such as "heaven" or "hell," "saved" or "unsaved," "demon" or "saint." This baggage will cause us to disregard, avoid, or even shun some of the answers wandering about the room while simultaneously causing us to gravitate toward others with admiration, curiosity, love, friendship, empathy, and compassion. We must drop this baggage! It is essential to keep this setting—that of a large party, feast, or celebration—in mind and heart as you read the following pages. In order to maintain a tone of discovery and love, it is also important to recognize your predispositions for certain perspectives and against others. You don't want to be the one who crashes the celebration with rudeness, judgment, or dishonor. You and I are guests in someone else's house. We do not have to agree with everyone at the party or with all of the views expressed on the following pages (if you did, you would be confused and not only look foolish but also be considered a fool), but we must remember we are all guests, gathered in the same room for a bit so we can get to know each other better in a safe, healthy way, through open dialogue and fruitful, meaningful conversation, through thoughtful questions and active, engaged listening.

Throughout this "party," try to get a sense of the overall tone and landscape of each worldview, each "person," and find points of commonality between yourself and each view. I encourage you to read with a pencil, pen, or highlighter and mark aspects that resonate with you or connect with what you believe to be true. When my students and friends do this, they often realize that what they thought they believed is vastly different from what is actually on their functional daily trust lists.

Let's move now into the first format to compare and contrast each view.

SEVEN ESSENTIAL QUESTIONS

1. What is the nature of reality? What is really real?

IDEALISM

A pure idealist trusts that only the spiritual is really real. Reality is a state of eternal spiritual perfection.

MATERIALISM

An authentic materialist trusts that only the material (the natural) is really real; there is no spiritual realm.

MONISM

A complete monist trusts that the spiritual and the material are both really real, existing as one entity without any actual distinction. Reality *presents* itself as dual with distinctions in nature, yet all of existence is ultimately one universal, inter-connected unity.

THEISM

A religious theist trusts that the spiritual and the material are both real, yet they are independent (self-reliant and separated from each other), interdependent (collaboratively and recipro-cally reliant on each other), and paradoxically intradependent (unified and reliant upon each other as a collective whole, like a body with integrated dependent parts).

2. Who or what is God?

IDEALISM

A pure idealist trusts that the impersonal, eternal, perfect spiritual ideal is what people often call "god." It is absolute, complete truth, beauty, and goodness.

MATERIALISM

An authentic materialist trusts there is no objective, powerful being outside of the material. God is a figment of man's creativity and imagination, a creative idea or concept.

MONISM

A complete monist trusts that everything is "god." Because there is no literal distinction between anything, there is no distinction between god and humans and the fabric of the universe. Everything and everybody in the universe is an integral, interconnected part of the unity of life called "god."

THEISM

A religious theist trusts there is a distinct God who is the all-powerful creator, sustainer, and giver of all of life. God is personal and has personality.

3. What is a human being? What is humankind? (Who am I? What am I?)

IDEALISM

A pure idealist trusts that humans exist as one of the infinite, incomplete, imperfect replicas or shadows of the real, eternal, ideal state of spiritual perfection.

MATERIALISM

An authentic materialist trusts that human beings are a fascinating, unique, and highly complex system of matter and electricity that is incredibly aware of self and others.

MONISM

A complete monist trusts that a human is a unique, unrepeatable part of "god." Humanity is part of the body of the universe and the entirety of reality referred to as "god."

THEISM

A religious theist trusts that humans are distinct, wonderful creations made for relationship with each other and God. Some religious theists believe that humans are made in the image of God but do not possess the exact nature of God, or they exist as merely an extension or simply as a part of God.

4. What is the basis of and standard for morality? How do I decide between right and wrong, and who or what is the basis for moral authority?

IDEALISM

A pure idealist trusts that all morality is objective and based on the nature of the impersonal, perfect, spiritual ideal, which is absolute truth, perfect beauty, and complete goodness.

MATERIALISM

An authentic materialist trusts that all morality is ultimately subjective and based exclusively or collectively on self, majority, and power.

MONISM

A complete monist trusts that morality is entirely subjective based solely on one's individual preference and as a part of the interconnected, universal reality called "god." Thus, morality is completely relative, yet it appears dual in nature due to the complexity, polarities, and variety found in the universe.

THEISM

A religious theist trusts that all ethical morality is objective based on the nature of God, who is perfection and goodness. God is the standard for and author of morality. Many sincere theists follow ritual moral codes pertaining to personal and collective religious beliefs, distinct from ethical moral codes.

5. What happens to humans at death?

IDEALISM

A pure idealist trusts that when a human dies, perfection is attained. The human "becomes" part of (or is "absorbed" or is "purified" into) a unified state of spiritual perfection and/or ceases to exist as a shadow of perfection and as an imperfect "self."

MATERIALISM

An authentic materialist trusts that humans cease to be aware of their existence at the point of death.

MONISM

A complete monist trusts that when a human dies, he or she literally morphs into another part of existence and another component of the universal reality, which is god.

THEISM

A religious theist trusts that when humans die, they either obtain and sustain individual perfection or "wholeness" and exist eternally in continual relationship with the perfect, personal God, or they remain in an imperfect, incomplete state and necessarily exist separated from God, who is perfect.

6. What is the meaning and purpose of human history? What is the essence of human interaction and relationships?

IDEALISM

A pure idealist trusts that history and human memory are records of humans striving to escape nonexistence and attain an ideal state of spiritual perfection.

MATERIALISM

According to James Sire in *The Universe Next Door*, an authentic materialist trusts that "history is a linear stream of events linked by cause and effect but without an overarching purpose"[2] (such as natural selection). Human interaction is chemistry, pure cause and effect.

MONISM

A complete monist trusts that history and human memory consist of the repository of the collective memories of our collective coexistence and consciousness as god.

THEISM

Again, James Sire says it well: a sincere theist trusts that "history is linear, a meaningful sequence of events leading to the fulfillment of God's purposes for humanity."[3] History is the true, epic adventure story of God's interaction with humankind; it is the real story of life humans are participating in.

7. Why are we here? Where are we going? What is the purpose of human existence? What is the purpose of living for tomorrow?

IDEALISM

A pure idealist trusts that humans exist only to achieve and sustain an ideal state of spiritual perfection.

MATERIALISM

An authentic materialist trusts that humans create their own individual and collective meaning for life.

MONISM

A complete monist trusts that every human has the exciting opportunity to experience being various components of universal reality—of god—forever.

THEISM

A sincere theist trusts that at least one reason humans exist is to enjoy and experience a meaningful relationship with God, the Creator and Sustainer of life.

CHAPTER 8

A Closer Look at Pure Idealism

A wise man, recognizing that the world is but an illusion,
does not act as if it is real, so he escapes the suffering.

ATTRIBUTED TO THE BUDDHA

Pure Idealism: *We are striving to exist as spiritual perfection, the spiritual ideal (as God or as part of God).*

Pure idealists trust that only the spiritual is the eternal fabric of Prime Reality. True idealists have a foundational understanding that the nonmaterial, perfect ideal has an eternal, beautiful, true, and good weight and realness to it that supersedes any physical attempt to replicate and materialize this true idea. It often helps to think of people adopting this worldview as "Idea-ists."

Let's try something. Think of your favorite car or chair. Why is this your favorite? What features make it the best? If you are in a chair or car, are you sitting in or riding in the ultimately *perfect* one right now? Does it have no flaws, nothing that can be improved, and nothing that will break or run down? Does such a thing even exist on our planet? Unfortunately, no. No one can point to a perfected car or chair in the physical realm. They all wear down—that chair that was so comfortable becomes less and less comfortable the more you sit in it. Your favorite car will need costly repairs and eventually will stop working altogether. We can all think of the idea of the perfect chair or car, and many of the car and chair companies (barring planned obsolescence) are striving to make the perfect car or chair. But alas! They have not done it yet.

Now consider this: were we to somehow rid the entire planet of every car and every chair, the *idea* of the perfect car and chair would still remain. Even without the physical objects, we could still imagine the ideal. There is much more to the discussion, but I think it will suffice for our purposes to simply add one more point. Now I want you to close your eyes and think of the perfect being (it can be a human being if you want). Contemplate this being—the ideal being who could be, for example, always true, perfectly kind, authentically loving, incredibly strong, flawlessly beautiful, with vibrant, perfect, uninterrupted health . . . did you imagine yourself as you are right now?

I've done this exercise with thousands of participants, youth and adults, from all over the world, no one—not one!—has ever said they had pictured themselves. If you did not picture yourself as currently perfect and flawless, welcome to idealism: you have an idea of the ideal, of perfection; you have admitted that you are not that ideal; thus, you are now ready to start your journey toward becoming this ideal. That is your "homework" for the rest of your life.

This understanding leads idealists to a greater awareness that the weight or realness of the ideal is manifested in a spiritual reality and is merely represented (re-presented), often poorly, in the physical. For idealists, this understanding applies to the entire physical world but particularly to humans. Humans are essentially imperfect shadows or incomplete imitations of the spiritual ideal. Humans are trying to become one with ultimate reality, which is an enlightened state of spiritual perfection. Currently, humans are imperfect and exist on earth only as representations or imperfect images of perfection. In essence, humans exist as potential. A pure idealist would say humans have the opportunity to achieve eternal existence in a state of perfection in the ideal spiritual realm. An honest idealist would also say this is a difficult achievement.

To further illustrate this abstract concept, take a moment to make a shadow in front of yourself. As you look at the shadow, consider these questions: Is the shadow real? What is the substance of the shadow—what is it made of? The shadow is totally dependent on whatever is making it, and what is making the shadow is not dependent on the shadow at all. The shadow exists, *if* it exists, because of the substance creating it, not vice versa. Try picking up the shadow with your hands or something else. Once again, welcome to idealism! With regard to this demonstration, what is creating the shadow represents the spiritual realm, and the shadow represents the material realm. If the shadow wants to exist forever, it must become the substance that is creating the shadow. Otherwise the shadow will cease to exist when the light changes.

Similarly, look at a photo of yourself. Try to imagine what the picture might have to do or might have to go through to actually become you (a living being) and not just an imperfect, incomplete image of you. For a pure idealist, humans are personally responsible for making themselves into the ideal, for becoming perfectly good, beautiful, and true, for becoming really real and not just an image of reality. In the spiritual state, individuals will exist fully and eternally as spiritual perfection. In so doing, they will eternally escape the fate of nonexistence as an incomplete, shadowy replica, trapped in the finite brokenness of the material realm.

Buddhism, Taoism, and much of Hinduism construct trust lists from the idealist worldview. If you are not a follower of one of those isms, take a moment and imagine how this big perspective on the nature of reality would instruct your overall outlook on life as well as your day-to-day choices. In the next few pages we will look at how idealism answers the seven big questions. You may also find it instructive to research idealist religions and isms further and have conversations with people who follow them.

ANSWERING THE BIG QUESTIONS OF LIFE: ANOTHER LOOK AT THE PHILOSOPHICAL TRUST LIST OF A PURE IDEALIST

1. What is the nature of reality? What is really real?

A pure idealist trusts that only the spiritual is really real and reality is a state of eternal, spiritual perfection. The material realm is an imperfect, incomplete, shadowy replica of the ideal. In other words, the material realm is a broken, twisted, and warped shadow of the ideal, which is absolutely good, perfectly beautiful, and purely true.

2. Who or what is God?

A pure idealist trusts that the impersonal, eternal, perfect, one ideal is what people call "god." It is absolute and complete truth, beauty, and goodness. God is a state of mind and a state of existence. God is the ideal one who is perfect, absolutely and forever. God is the ideal state of being that is the pursuit of humanity.

3. What is a human being? What is humankind? (Who am I? What am I?)

A pure idealist trusts that humans are not perfect; they are one of the infinite, incomplete shadows of the real state of spiritual perfection. Humans exist simply as potential to become one with the ideal and to finally exist as the perfected ideal in a state of eternal, spiritual perfection and completeness.

4. What is the basis of and standard for morality? How do I decide between right and wrong, and who or what is the basis for moral authority?

A pure idealist trusts that all morality is objective, based on the nature of the impersonal, perfect spiritual ideal, which is absolute truth, perfect beauty, and complete goodness. All thought and behavior is aimed at achieving and sustaining this state of existence.

5. What happens to humans at death?

A pure idealist trusts that when humans die, perfection is attained and unity with the ideal is achieved. Humans realize their potential, let go of the imperfect representation of self, and become one with the state of spiritual perfection. They cease to exist as imperfect selves and shadowy, broken representations of perfection. They cease to exist materially on earth. Individually, humans cease to exist at all. In essence, real life/ true existence begins at death. Philosophically speaking, the imperfect transient shadow fades, and only the eternal ideal remains. (Religions that have adopted beliefs such as reincarnation and the Karma cycle provide the opportunity for continued chances and attempts at achieving the ideal state for those who do not achieve it.)

6. What is the meaning and purpose of human history? What is the essence of human interaction and relationships?

A pure idealist trusts that history and memory are a record of humans striving to escape nonexistence and attain an ideal state of spiritual perfection. Human interaction is summed up and actualized in striving to escape nonexistence, either alone or together.

7. Why are we here? Where are we going? What is the purpose of human existence? What is the purpose of living for tomorrow?

A pure idealist trusts that humans exist only to achieve and sustain an ideal state of spiritual perfection, to escape painful nonexistence, and to exist eternally through becoming absorbed into/unified with the spiritual ideal, which is absolutely, perfectly good, beautiful, and true.

CHAPTER 9

A Closer Look at Authentic Materialism

And when I feel, fair creature of an hour!
That I shall never look upon thee more,
Never have relish in the faery power
Of unreflecting love!—then on the shore
Of the wide world I stand alone, and think,
Till Love and Fame to nothingness do sink.

JOHN KEATS

Authentic Materialism: *We are our own individual gods; there is no objective God to become, to serve, to submit to, or to dwell with. We simply are.*

Authentic materialists trust that the composition of Prime Reality is only that which can be observed and measured materially. No real spirituality or spiritual realm exists. Humans are beautiful, complex systems of matter and electricity who are subjected to an intricate arrangement of pure cause and effect and who are aware of their immediate, unfolding presence in time and space. To wrap one's mind around the tenets of materialism, it is essential to imagine our world as one gigantic system of electrical impulses. Electrons give movement to formations of matter and, therefore, give the perception or definition of "life" to certain objects. It is like a toy with batteries. No batteries, no life.

To help grasp this, think of the elemental differences between a computer and your body. For an authentic materialist, this ends up being merely a matter of perception and substance; it is quantitative, not qualitative. If the computer runs out of electricity, we add more; if it breaks, we fix it; if we can't or don't want to fix it, we recycle the parts or toss it in the trash pile. An authentic materialist quickly recognizes (without shame or fear) that this is exactly the same with a human body. If you were to run out of electricity, you would need to get more. If you pass out and stop moving due to a heart attack, someone would need to grab an automated external defibrillator, put the patches on your chest, yell, "Clear!" and press the button to pump some electricity through your body so it can potentially reboot and recalibrate and possibly keep running. If not, the next option would be to try to fix you, and if that won't work and materialism is what is really going on in the universe, you might share any of your working parts with whoever needs them, because *you* won't need them anymore. From this basic understanding of zero spirituality and the foundational principle of there being no objective creator, the rest of materialism naturally falls into place. The other six questions answer themselves logically.

In materialism, the impression of perfection or of the spiritual ideal is a completely subjective, relative concept. Consistent materialists believe that humans can do and be whatever they prefer, so long as they avoid negative natural consequences.

Simultaneously and paradoxically, a consistent materialist acknowledges that this freedom is arbitrary and that it is ultimately a facade. Life is actually an unfolding, passive adventure of random, electric, reactionary impulses.

This was beautifully illustrated to me when my twins and I watched a compelling nature show called *Planet Earth* produced by the BBC. This particular episode showed a helicopter shot of millions of caribou roaming across the tundra.[1] We were in awe of the spectacle of so much life walking in powerful unity. My mind drifted to a favorite line of poetry from "The Fall of Rome": "Altogether elsewhere . . . Silently and very fast."[2]

I was jerked out of my poetry daydream by a squeal. "No! Run, baby caribou, run!" My daughter Anna, snuggled deep into my left armpit, was shouting at the television. A short-legged baby caribou, through no particular fault of his own, had become separated from the herd and was being left behind.

The tension escalated when out of the bottom corner of the screen a wolf appeared. "Wolf!" Elijah, Anna's twin brother, cheered. "Go, wolf! Go, wolf!" Elijah started chanting at the screen on my right side.

"Run, baby caribou! Run!" screamed Anna from my left.

This is it, I thought, *the essence of materialism*. All of life wrapped up in a cause-and-effect, life-or-death struggle. No choices, no morality, no autonomy—just reactions and causes and more reactions and causes, the unfolding of electrons and chemistry interacting. Who am I to impose morality or judgment on the baby caribou or the wolf? Both are simply doing what they do—as all of us are doing every day all over the planet. Cause and effect, chemical and electrical impulse, life-or-death struggle. Anna started weeping when we heard the little caribou squeal as the wolf attacked it (off screen—thank you, *Planet Earth*), and Elijah jumped up and gave a mighty fist pump of victory and a deep, powerful, "Yes, wolf!"

A pure materialist simply observes what is unfolding all around without judgment—simply observes and becomes aware of the unfolding mystery of life.

Consistent and authentic materialists unabashedly and wholeheartedly embrace the idea that life is ultimately absurd and beautifully or grotesquely ridiculous. Therefore, genuine materialists assert that humans can attempt to create their own sense of adventure, purpose, and meaning. Humans live out their awareness in the most personally pleasurable ways available while seeking to achieve positive natural consequences and avoid negative natural consequences.

Below is a list of some religions, isms, and ways that construct trust lists from this worldview. With this information in mind, you can learn more about why people of these particular religions and isms make the choices they make concerning day-to-day living and lifestyles. You may find it instructive to further research these and have some conversations with people who have adopted these lifestyles:

+ Atheism
+ Humanism
+ Materialistic existentialism
+ Phenomenology
+ Nihilism

ANSWERING THE BIG QUESTIONS OF LIFE: ANOTHER LOOK AT THE PHILOSOPHICAL TRUST LIST OF AN AUTHENTIC MATERIALIST

1. What is the nature of reality? What is really real?

An authentic materialist trusts that only the material (the natural) is really real; there is no spiritual realm. Matter and electricity have existed eternally in various forms and states without beginning or end. What is observable and measurable is really real.

The spiritual realm can be a figment of the human imagination caused by chemical or electrical reactions in the human imagination. The so-called "spiritual" can represent all humans have yet to discover, measure, and understand.

2. Who or what is God?

An authentic materialist trusts that there is no external creator god in the universe. When the general definition and attributes of god (meaning the god others believe in) are investigated, they are revealed as either unreal ideas or as amplified human characteristics.

There is no objective, powerful being outside of the material. God is a lovely or ugly lie, a figment of man's creativity and imagination, or a generative creative idea or concept.

3. What is a human being? What is humankind? (Who am I? What am I?)

An authentic materialist trusts that a human being is a fascinating, unique, and highly complex system of matter and electricity that is uniquely aware of self and others.

Humankind is currently the pinnacle of existence in an infinitely intricate system of cause and effect. Humankind is the amazing realization of the ongoing potential of matter and electricity.

4. What is the basis of and standard for morality? How do I decide between right and wrong, and who or what is the basis for moral authority?

An authentic materialist trusts that all morality is ultimately subjective and based on self, majority, and/or power. Morality is essentially absurd at the core. There is no truly objective standard for good and evil for humans, nor could there ever be. Therefore, all morality is essentially relative, based on value and agreed submission to (or rejection of) a constructed system of human authority, community, and power. Furthermore, a consistent materialist will acknowledge that the complete lack of free will means there must also be a lack of culpability, and this adds another layer of absurdity to the idea of morality.

5. What happens to humans at death?

An authentic materialist trusts that humans cease to be aware of their existence at the point of death. There is no eternal existence of a person's "soul" beyond the grave because there is no eternal soul dwelling in the human body. Real life ends at death.

6. What is the meaning and purpose of human history? What is the essence of human interaction and relationships?

An authentic materialist trusts that humans, individually or collectively, create their own meaning for existence.

History and memory are ultimately absurd with no objective, overarching meaning or purpose. To quote James Sire, "History is a linear stream of events linked by cause and effect but without an overarching purpose"[3] in a closed system (such as natural selection). All human interaction is chemistry and pure cause and effect.

7. Why are we here? Where are we going? What is the purpose of human existence? What is the purpose of living for tomorrow?

An authentic materialist trusts that humans create their own meaning for life. At the core, life is essentially, objectively absurd because no objective meaning or purpose does or can exist.

Humans live for whatever brings pleasure or the hope of pleasure.

Humans hope for or strive to create beneficial changes in their circumstances with the goal of increasing positive natural consequences and decreasing negative natural consequences.

A Closer Look at Complete Monism

The entire system of the universe, visible and invisible, is the scene of a great scheme of evolution, in which life moves to ever more expressive form, more responsive awareness, and more unified consciousness. The human consciousness . . . is in essence identical with the one supreme Reality, which Ralph Waldo Emerson called the "Oversoul," including each of our particular beings and uniting us with one another.

THE THEOSOPHICAL SOCIETY IN AMERICA

Complete Monism: *We are already part of god (the universe). Embrace and enjoy this truth and stop striving to become what you already are.*

Complete monists trust that both the measurable material and mysterious spiritual realms coexist as one (very large) entity. Monists, often called pantheists, assert that all of reality is one reality presenting itself as dual in nature. This duality, or apparent duality, is represented in unlimited perspectives and polarities as experienced throughout the vast complexity and tensions of life. It can be helpful to think of monism as "mono-ism." *Mono* means "one"; thus, monism is "one-ism."

After reading this text, Marti MacCullough, a friend and philosophy mentor of mine, pointed out that, according to the guiding principles of the literal meaning of *monism*, idealism and materialism could both be considered monistic. Materialism holds that all of reality is one reality, and this reality is only the material. Materialism, like monism, posits that the universe is one gigantic, interconnected whole, with the significant difference being that the entirety of the universe is composed of the periodic table of elements. The same is true for idealism, except that the "one essence" is spiritual. Marti and I pondered the implications of this realization for quite some time. The most fruitful outcome of our pondering was the realization that the only worldview that can authentically allow for any real relationship is theism, for although it asserts connection between the spiritual and the material, it also allows for real distinction between the two.

I asked Marti for a better term to use. Neither of us could think of one, particularly because the word *monism* helps people understand the driving principle of this worldview: the two realities of the spiritual and the material are believed to be literally one entity. Let me take a moment to compare and contrast theism and monism. For theists, this exercise usually creates the "aha" moment much needed at this point.

Most theists believe humans have a spirit. The Bible is crystal clear on this issue. For example, there are many psalms (particularly 42) in which David talks to his own spirit within him. Christians take this one step further and trust even that God's Spirit resides within them. A passage from the apostle Paul's letter to the church at Corinth helps drive home this point. He refers to the human body as "the temple of the Holy Spirit" (1 Corinthians 6:19). Thus, Bible-believing Christians trust

that God's unifying, undivided Holy Spirit indwells humans—
while each human also maintains the dignity of an individual
human spirit. One way to say this is that each of our bodies is a
temple for our own human spirit to inhabit and also the temple
where God's Holy Spirit takes up residence. For Christians it is
like sharing an apartment with a powerful roommate!

This understanding is often helpful for both monists and
theists alike—because the language overlaps so much. Theism
believes each individual human body has a unique soul that
makes me *me* and you *you*. But as Paul writes, the Spirit of
God can also indwell a person, manifesting himself in different gifts unique to each person but also working as a unifying
and connecting presence among people. Therefore, there is a
unique, paradoxical unity-distinction in Christian theism. I will
explain this further in part 3, but it is helpful to touch on it here
because this helps theists understand monism's idea of the one,
unifying spirit indwelling everything. Unlike theism, though,
monism has no paradox, for in monism, there are no individual
spirits. Nothing separates humans from the one unifying spirit
in all humans; therefore, humans are not distinguished from
each other spiritually.

A conversation with my three oldest children—Anna,
Eli, and Olivia—illuminates the spiritual difference between
monism and theism. I asked them, "As Christians, do we believe
that we each have a different human spirit? A part of you that is
uniquely you? An Anna-spirit? An Eli-spirit? An Olivia-spirit? A
Matthew-spirit?" As religious theists, they nodded in agreement,
and I responded, "Yes—four distinct human spirits. Okay, then,
do you have the Holy Spirit of God dwelling within you?" As
Christ-centered theists, they nodded again. "Do I have the same

God Spirit within me?" More nods. I said, "Good, I agree. Yes, I do. Are there four different God Spirits, one in each of us?"

They began to shake their heads now, and Anna said, "There is only one Spirit of God, but it's God's Spirit in all of us, uniting all of us."

And in response, I said, "Now, if you want to understand monism, take the individual, unique human spirit out of each of our bodies and what is left?"

Livi shouted, "God!" Even five-year-old Olivia understands the distinction between her own spirit and God's Spirit within her. Just as King David once asked why his own soul within him was "discouraged" and then told his soul to "hope in God," Olivia may also someday have the same question, acknowledging her human spirit as separate from and still capable of being influenced by God's Spirit (Psalm 43:5).

I hope this helped the light bulb come on for you. If it's still a bit dim, consider this summary: in monism, god's spirit is in each of us; there is no individual human spirit; god's spirit is what is really living. So basically, I am god. And so are you. And god is what is moving me and connecting all things. God's spirit is what is animating our bodies with the various things we do each day because in each body god is what god does. And since there is only one spirit of god in all of us, we are all connected. Actually, a helpful way to think of it is to think of the universe as god's body. And because god is so big, of course his body would need to be as big as the universe—one big universe that is all connected, just like any individual body is connected, having different parts but all connected as one body, and one big god spirit giving it life.

Thus, for a complete monist, all of life is connected. Humans are part of all existence, and all of what exists is already the ideal for life. Thus, humans are already perfect as various parts of the one entity that monists often refer to as god. God literally is everything, and humans are part of the everything that exists. For all of life:

Emotions = Spirit = God = Truth = Life = Material = Perspective = Emotions

Like any human body that has many apparent distinctions and parts yet maintains a complex unity and harmony, so is the universal reality and unity of monism. Humans each embody unique perspectives of god (the everything). Humans have unlimited potential and power as god or as a connected part of god. Humans embrace their unique preferences and seek a balance of all perspectives and polarities so as to wake up, realize, and utilize their true identity and unity. Humans (along with all creatures and all parts of reality) grow in awareness of all perspectives as they embody the simplicity and complexities of life as part of the one, gigantic self. Humans learn how to see all of life and all of life's tensions and polarities—the dualities of life—as a valid and valuable part of humanity's collective unity and coexistence with all that exists.

Here is a list of some religions, isms, and ways that construct trust lists from this worldview:

+ Pantheism
+ New Age
+ Much of Hinduism
+ Spiritual existentialism

+ Tribal religions that worship nature
+ Theosophy

ANSWERING THE BIG QUESTIONS OF LIFE: ANOTHER LOOK AT THE PHILOSOPHICAL TRUST LIST OF A COMPLETE MONIST

1. What is the nature of reality? What is really real?

A complete monist trusts that the spiritual and the material are both real, existing as one entity.

The spiritual realm and material realm both exist, but they are one and the same. What we call distinctions and separation are illusory; there is no actual separation or distinction.

Reality presents itself as dual in nature through polarity and perspectives. However, all of existence is ultimately one universal, interconnected unity unfolding in various forms.

2. Who or what is God?

A complete monist trusts that everything is god. Everything and everybody in the universe is an integral, interconnected part of the unity of life called god.

Existence and reality are what people often call god. The cosmos is filled with duality and polarity as manifested in all of life (birth and death, dark and light, hot and cold, creation and destruction, etc.); thus, god has a dual nature in essence and in being.

3. What is a human being? What is humankind? (Who am I? What am I?)

A complete monist trusts that humans are unique, unrepeatable parts of god. Humanity is part of the body of the universe and the entirety of reality appropriately referred to as god. The spiritual component to reality resides within, flows through, and permeates every human.

Humans are not truly distinct and separate from god, but humans exist as part of the material and spiritual reality of the cosmos, which, in essence, is part of the entire being of god.

4. What is the basis of and standard for morality? How do I decide between right and wrong, and who or what is the basis for moral authority?

A complete monist trusts that morality is completely subjective, based solely on one's individual preference as a part of the interconnected, universal reality called god. Like god (as god is manifested in the universe), morality is dual in nature. That is to say, god and morality are positive and negative energy, creative and destructive forces, darkness and light, heat and cold, and so on, ad infinitum.

5. What happens to humans at death?

A complete monist trusts that when a human dies, that person morphs into another part of existence and another component of reality, which is god. The shared, united soul shifts into another part of the cosmos with another unique perspective on living as god.

6. What is the meaning and purpose of human history? What is the essence of human interaction and relationships?

A complete monist trusts that history and memory consist of the repository of the memories of our collective coexistence as god. Humans are connected to history as part of the eternally unfolding story of the cosmos (which is god).

7. Why are we here? Where are we going? What is the purpose of human existence? What is the purpose of living for tomorrow?

A complete monist trusts that every human has the exciting opportunity to continually experience being various components of universal reality—of god—forever. Each human is here to wake up to who he or she is as a unique part of god and reach full potential as a distinct part of the divine existence and unity of god.

CHAPTER 11

A Closer Look at Religious Theism

What comes into our minds when we think about God
is the most important thing about us.

A. W. TOZER

Religious Theism: *We are unique, individual creations
hoping to become perfect (or complete) so as to dwell with
God, our perfect Creator.*

Sincere theists trust that both the spiritual and the material are
components of Prime Reality. While they are interdependent
and dependent on the other, they are also mysteriously intradependent, or dependent *within* each other. Humans are unique,
individual creations in the image of a free, independent, personal, and powerful Creator, commonly referred to as God.

Although humans are made in the image of God as individual, distinct creations of God, humans are independent beings
from God and do not possess the exact nature of God. Humans
are created to dwell freely with God and to enjoy some form of
relationship with God and God's creation. I have yet to find a
type of theism that has a God who does not possess personality,

being, and creativity, nor am I aware of a type of theism that has a God who is not the standard for and author of morality for humanity. Humans are not more powerful than God, and they are created beings, not the Creator. (I have already addressed the issue of who God is for polytheists in chapter 5 and will not unpack that again here.)

It is challenging to not slip into religious talk in a chapter like this. Many philosophy texts and worldview curricula end up as platforms for comparative religion. I am fine with comparative religion—those texts and classes are helpful as we navigate our world—but that is not the aim of this text. In this text, and particularly this section, I want to focus on what unites these various religions and what is behind and motivating their religious principles and practices. I have found it most fruitful to have genuine, healthy, safe, and open conversations with real people who really believe the tenets of these various religions; then it is essential to read the primary texts of these various religions. I have been on, and continue to be on, that very intriguing and eye-opening adventure of learning. For example, I had to accept that many "native" and tribal religions are practically theistic, and not monistic. Many people lump tribal religions together as monistic, but simply asking who or what god is and what a human is can help us see very clear delineations. The Sioux, for example, have a creation story of humanity and a creator God that is similar to monotheistic creation accounts in the Bible and the Koran. Look at the primary texts for yourself:

> So God created human beings in his own image. In the image of God he created them; male and female he created them.
>
> GENESIS 1:27

Verily We created man from a product of wet earth;
then placed him as a drop (of seed) in a safe lodging;
then We fashioned the drop into a clot, then We
fashioned the clot into a little lump, then We fashioned
the little lump into bones, then clothed the bones with
flesh, and then produced it another creation. So blessed
be Allah, the Best of Creators!

KORAN SURAH 23:12-14

I am a red man. If the Great Spirit had desired me to
be a white man he would have made me so in the first
place. He put in your heart certain wishes and plans, in
my heart he put other and different desires. Each man
is good in his sight. It is not necessary for Eagles to be
Crows. We are poor . . . but we are free.

SITTING BULL, HUNKPAPA LAKOTA SIOUX

One of the most important aspects of philosophical theism
is found in those last few words from Sitting Bull: "We are free."
Freedom and free will, distinction and some level of autonomy,
are the only things that make relationship possible, and these
critical issues are what make theism distinct from the other
three worldviews. C. S. Lewis says it like this:

God created things which had free will. That means
creatures which can go either wrong or right. Some
people think they can imagine a creature which was
free but had no possibility of going wrong; I cannot. If
a thing is free to be good it is also free to be bad. And
free will is what has made evil possible. Why, then, did
God give them free will? Because free will, though it

makes evil possible, is also the only thing that makes possible any love or goodness or joy worth having. A world of automata—of creatures that worked like machines—would hardly be worth creating.[1]

To highlight this freedom and relationship and to illustrate how humans are unique creations of a God with being and personality (not just consciousness or a state of being), I consider the painting of the *Creation of Adam* from the ceiling of the Sistine Chapel. I know that this is distinctly Christian, but the metaphor would work for anyone who has a theistic worldview. In the painting there is a very muscular, bearded God hovering in a red backdrop and surrounded by chubby cherubs, extending his arm out and down to an equally muscular Adam who is reposed on something like a rock. The most essential piece of the painting for our purposes here is the inch of separation and distinction. These two beings are almost touching but not quite. There is relationship in their eyes, facial expression, reach, and movement. There are obvious distinctions such as beard and garment. But what are most powerful to me are the similarities. I can't tell who has the bigger biceps or quads; they both have eyes, ears, and mouths. They look like they could wrestle, converse, go for a walk, and share a tasty beverage or scrumptious meal together. They look like they could be best friends and talk until the sun comes up or maybe not talk at all. Adam and God could hug if they wanted to. A Buddhist cannot hug nirvana, and a Hindu cannot have a conversation and a meal with Brahma. I am not saying that in theism God will necessarily hug you, share a conversation with you, or enjoy a meal with you. Nevertheless, in theism God is a relational being, and in order for God to have relationship, there must be something to have a relationship with.

Part of this relationship is that most religious theists believe that on earth, humans exist as imperfect, incomplete beings, essentially separated from God's perfect identity and standards. Therefore, in order for these "incomplete" humans to escape eternal separation from their perfect Creator and to dwell perpetually in relationship with their perfect Creator, individual perfection and fullness must be achieved or received and sustained. The various and numerous religions, denominations, ways, and isms of theism offer countless options, explanations, and ideas describing the current relationship between God and humans and what is necessary in order to be in and sustain a relationship with God.

Below is a list of some of the major religions, isms, and ways that construct trust lists from this worldview. Like Buddhism and Hinduism, the following have multitudinous denominations and sects within their religions:

+ Judaism
+ Islam
+ Christianity
+ Tribal religions that worship a creator

ANSWERING THE BIG QUESTIONS OF LIFE: ANOTHER LOOK AT THE PHILOSOPHICAL TRUST LIST OF A SINCERE THEIST

1. What is the nature of reality? What is really real?

A sincere theist trusts that the spiritual and the material are both real, yet they are independent of and interdependent on each other. The spiritual realm and material realm are both independently real, yet they coexist and interact independently, interdependently, and intradependently within each other in various forms and degrees and in diverse ways.

2. Who or what is God?

A religious theist trusts that there is a God who is the all-powerful creator, the sustainer, and the giver of all life. God is perfect and essentially good in nature and being. God is personal and has a personality. God has full authority. God is the standard for and author of morality.

3. What is a human being? What is humankind? (Who am I? What am I?)

A religious theist trusts that humans are distinct yet dependent, wonderful creations made in the image of God, or at least capable of some type of meaningful relationship with God; however, humans do not possess the exact nature of God, nor do they exist as only an extension or merely a part of God.

4. What is the basis of and standard for morality? How do I decide between right and wrong, and who or what is the basis for moral authority?

A religious theist trusts that all ethical morality is objective, based on the personal, all-powerful nature of God, who is perfect and good. God is the standard for and author of morality, as are God's word and God's nature. Though this does not necessarily have to, this may include ritual traditions or cultural norms—what many would call "ritual morality," which is uniquely distinct from ethical morality.

5. What happens to humans at death?

A religious theist trusts that when a human dies, one of two things will occur based on God's and the human's choices in this life. Either the person will obtain or will have received individual perfection and exist eternally in continual relationship with the perfect, personal God, or this person will remain in an imperfect, incomplete state and necessarily exist separated from God. When humans die, they either actualize their true self and exist (or continue to exist) with God or are eternally separated from perfection and wholeness. For most religious theists, real life is both now and later; reality, and thus some form of relationship with God, is available in this life and continues after death.

6. What is the meaning and purpose of human history? What is the essence of human interaction and relationships?

A religious theist, according to James Sire, trusts that history is "linear, a meaningful sequence of events leading to the fulfillment of God's purposes for humanity" in an open system.[2] History is the true, epic adventure story of God's interaction with humankind. It is the real story humans are in right now. Humans are independent and dependent, possessing will and identity as self in communion with others.

7. Why are we here? Where are we going? What is the purpose of human existence? What is the purpose of living for tomorrow?

A religious theist trusts that at least one primary reason humans exist is to enjoy and experience some form of a meaningful relationship with the Creator and sustainer of life.

For Christian theists, humans exist in order to expand, enjoy, and protect God's Kingdom. They exist to bring joy and honor to God and self through genuine worship of God; through loving, healthy relationships with God and others; and through the authentic serving of God and others.

Judaism, Islam, and tribal religions that worship a Creator have similar ways to describe why humans were created. Of course, these other descriptions have their own flavor, subtleties, and nuances. I offer you my Christian perspective here to highlight that, as created beings, humans actually have purpose and meaning. It would be foolish for me to try to craft and condense statements like these about religions that are not my own. There are thousands of denominations in Christianity, and I am sure that some Christians will not agree with what I have written here. It would be presumptuous of me to think I could do this with another's religion. Again, the key is not that I get these statements right; the key for this philosophical approach to worldview is that in theism, this type of statement on meaning and purpose *can* actually have been written.

CHAPTER 12

My Trust List, Revisited

We've now looked at the four main worldviews and the way they would answer the seven big questions of this text. Now it's time for you to ponder your own answers to the seven questions, to think about your own trust list. The seven questions are listed on the next few pages for you to answer. Before you write down your thoughts, though, you may want to look back at all of part 2, paying close attention to any phrases you may have underlined or highlighted, any sentences or paragraphs that particularly impacted you. Another thing that might help you to honestly and thoughtfully answer the big questions is to have someone interview you. You may also want to carve out some solitude by going for a walk or finding a quiet place to sit and contemplate. Remember, the most important part of answering these big questions is that you do so with integrity and honesty.

BIG QUESTIONS AND BIG ANSWERS
OF LIFE FOR ME

1. What is the nature of reality? What is really real? Consider both the material and the spiritual realms.

2. Who or what is God?

3. What is a human being? What is humankind? (Who am I? What am I?)

4. What is the basis of and standard for morality? How do I decide between right and wrong, and who or what is the basis for moral authority?

5. What happens to humans at death? What do I trust will happen when I die?

6. What is the meaning and purpose of human history? What is the essence of human interaction and relationships?

7. Why are we here? Why am I here? Where are we going? Where am I going with my life? What is the purpose of living for tomorrow? What do I exist for?

PART THREE

Christ:
The Fullness
of Reality

CHAPTER 13

Open Our Eyes
So We Can See

We are now in the third part of this text. Before we move forward, let us review the action thus far. In part 1, we established that all our beliefs are based on trust. They cannot be proven and verified with 100 percent certitude, so you and I, like everyone else, are living life based on trust. In part 2, we looked at the four basic worldviews and how they answer some of the essential questions all humans ask. You also identified your own position within these views.

Now it is time to do some evaluation of the four worldviews. Before we embark on this, I want to warn you that this process will likely involve some pain and struggle. It is not easy to take the hammer of philosophy to the worldview you hold dear, to pull up its floors and open up its walls and do a close examination of it. But it is incredibly important to do this.

If you have not read Plato's allegory of the cave recently—or ever—I suggest you do, for he describes a process of examination and discovery much like the one we are on. Here, for our purposes, is a brief summary. The scene is that of people who have spent their entire lives chained, by feet and neck, inside a cave, facing a blank wall. Behind them is a great fire and beyond that is the exit from the cave leading to the outside world, to the sun, grass, trees, and so on. The chained people, however, have never seen either the fire or the outside world. All they have seen are shadows on the cave wall in front of them. They believe these shadows are reality. Plato argues that if these people were unchained and turned around and moved progressively toward the actual firelight and then beyond that to the outside and the sunshine, this journey would be difficult. Their eyes would be dazzled, their senses overwhelmed. They would argue it was all a dream. They would believe reality is the shadowy images reflected on the cave wall and these new sights are mere fantasies. They would say the truth was what they had before. Andrea Lunsford, in *The Presence of Others*, states, "Plato argues that this movement from darkness to light is like the journey the soul must make from the prison of mere sensory impressions (appearances or images) to the freedom of true reality, which exists only beyond the realm of the senses."[1]

Though I am not holding Plato's idea up as reality, I do believe his allegory accurately describes the journey we are taking in examining our own worldviews and the worldviews of others. The light of the fire—and then the sun—is dazzling. It hurts our eyes, and we are tempted to retreat to the only "reality" we've known, for it is safe and comfortable. If we settle for an unexamined "reality," though, we are trying to content ourselves with shadows cast by dim light, while the sun shines outside the cave. "Better," says Plato, "to be the poor servant of a poor master, and to endure anything, rather than . . . entertain these false notions and live in this miserable manner."[2]

Lunsford goes on to say, "In Plato's system, what we can see with our eyes is suspect, a mere shadow; only what we can see with our souls is 'real.' In making this argument, Plato raises issues as old as Western history. What is 'real,' and what is only apparently real? Which is more valuable, and why?"[3]

In contrast to Plato's view of reality is the picture presented in the Bible in 2 Kings 6. The prophet Elisha and his servant are trapped in a city surrounded by an enemy army. The servant is terrified, but Elisha is calm. The servant doesn't understand how Elisha can be so at peace. Doesn't Elisha see the great army camped around the city? What the servant doesn't understand is that he is seeing only partial reality. What he thinks is the complete truth is not, and this puts him in great darkness, despair, and fear. Out of this fear the servant says, "Oh, sir, what will we do now?" (verse 15), his only line in the entire story. (I am sure that could be colorfully translated if someone wanted to take the risk!) Elisha explains to the servant that there is a reality he (the servant) cannot see. Elisha tells him, "There are more on our side than on theirs" (verse 16). I'm sure there was an awkward pause here as the servant stared hard at the enemy army before turning back to Elisha with a very odd look. Elisha doesn't bother explaining; rather, he prays! And his prayer seems a little unusual for the circumstances. He doesn't pray, "O God, please send your army!" Or "O God, please rescue us in some creative and unique way!" No, Elisha prays, "O LORD, open his eyes and let him see!" (verse 17). Elisha prays for the servant's eyes to be opened! This probably prompted another strange look on the servant's face. He already has his eyes open! He can see the trouble—it's right there! Seeing it even more clearly isn't going to help him feel any better. We don't know if he communicated any of that to Elisha—he has only one line recorded in the story—but we can imagine it's what he is thinking.

But then God answers Elisha's prayer. He opens the servant's already-open eyes so that he, too, can see *all* of reality, not just part of it. The physical enemy army is still there—it *is* real—but what is also real are the spiritual horses and chariots of fire that surround the enemy. Plato argued that what we see with physical eyes is not actually real, but this scene in the Bible makes it clear that in the biblical view, *both* the physical *and* the spiritual are real and true. When the servant can see both material and spiritual reality, his perspective changes. And so does his emotional state. Again, our perceptions of and beliefs in Prime Reality directly correspond to our daily experience within Prime Reality. In this particular instance, Elisha's perception and understanding of reality spared him the trauma and fear his servant experienced.

John, in the opening of his Gospel, calls Jesus "the true light, who gives light to everyone," the true light who "shines in the darkness" and is not overcome by it (John 1:5, 9, NIV). Jesus, paradoxically, both sheds light on reality and is himself the fullness of reality. John also calls Jesus "life" and "glory" and says he is full of "grace and truth." It is my sincere belief that Jesus is the fullness of reality, but we have taken bits and pieces of this fullness and parceled it out, building entire worldviews on just one scrap. Perhaps the fullness is too dazzling, too overwhelming for us, and so our splitting apart this fullness is an attempt at controlling our perceptions of reality, a way of feeling safe and comfortable. Chesterton says we have "torn the soul of Christ into silly strips," with each strip holding only a portion of the truth.[4] If we want to make any steps toward seeing the fullness of reality, we must examine this idea. This is what we will do in this final part. We will examine the "strip" held by each worldview as well as the consequences of believing that this one strip is the whole. And, following the loving example of Jesus, we will do this in grace. We will pursue both grace and truth—together.

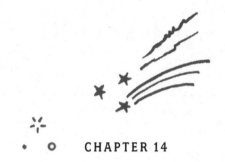

CHAPTER 14

Connecting Truth

Examination of worldviews often creates a combative atmosphere, as if those holding different worldviews are necessarily in conflict. Since one of the keys of this book is honor and integrity, and therefore we conduct our conversations "in a gentle and respectful way" (1 Peter 3:16), we want to carefully avoid an atmosphere of religious jousting. Remember, we want this to feel like a party—and none of us wants to ruin the party by being rude! Furthermore, this is a philosophical approach to worldview, not a religious approach. In our attempt to be gracious in our pursuit of truth, we are going to extend the metaphor of Chesterton's silly strips and think of reality as a painting, specifically Leonardo da Vinci's painting *The Last Supper*, one of the most beloved, studied, and replicated paintings in the world. Now, imagine something horrible: before the world ever saw *The Last Supper* in its entirety, someone close to da Vinci got his hands on a hammer and a chisel and started demolishing the wall where this magnificent painting was directly applied. This conniving entrepreneur then cut it into four vertical sections and sent each section to a different art collector, giving them the idea that their section was a complete painting on its own. This would be a terrible thing: first, that the masterful painting would be chopped up; and, second, that the pieces would be presented as complete entities. Yes, each section would still display da Vinci's magnificent skill; each would have a portion of the table, which extends across the length of the painting; and the colors in each section would still be varied and beautiful. But observers would miss the perspective gained only when viewing the painting in its entirety.

In this metaphor, it is essential to maintain the idea that the four pieces of the painting are from the original; they are original themselves. Yet what is also clear is that each section, or strip, even the one including Jesus Christ, is incomplete on its own, incapable of telling the entire story of the painting. Viewers would not even be aware there was more to the painting, but perhaps they might wonder about the rest of the room beyond what is included in their particular section—about who is being pointed to, about the rest of the person whose arm was included in their portion, about how long the table is. These questions would cause viewers to make assumptions, and some of these assumptions would certainly be wrong, for although each section *is* part of the original, it is still only part, and any attempt to describe the entire painting based on only one section of it would fail.

Yet this is what each worldview does. Each takes one strip or section and creates an entire view of reality based only on that one piece. The one piece of truth is not enough, of course, to support a view of all of life or reality, so each worldview adds to the strip to make up for what is lacking. The truth is there, but much has been added to it.

I want to be clear here in saying that these sections or strips are distinct from one another. They are not simply different expressions of one vague truth; no, they are discrete segments of the whole, with the whole being greater than the sum of the parts. What we will attempt in this section is to identify the truth held by each worldview and then look at some of what has been artificially added to try to complete the picture. We are, in essence, "collecting" truths and stripping away the additions. Eventually, with all the truths in hand, we can begin to piece back together the full painting. We can reconnect the truth; we can begin to see the *unity* of all truth.

I have at times been accused of vague or veiled pluralism in my efforts to treat all worldviews with dignity and honor. But I am not a pluralist. There is a huge difference between saying, "All worldviews contain parts that are true" and saying, "All worldviews *are* true." There is also a difference between saying, "All things are based on trust" and saying, "All things are trustworthy." It is similar to the difference between admitting that nothing is verifiable with 100 percent certitude and stating that nothing is reliable or trustworthy. The law of noncontradiction and the law of natural consequences will not allow the four different worldviews (which are based on different approaches to reality) to end up in pluralism because by nature they are not the same thing, nor are they *saying* the same thing.

I have made my position clear: I view the undivided person of Christ as the fullness of reality, the complete painting. He fills the whole, yet he makes room for each of us. When we see all of Christ, we can make better sense of all of reality, and we can make better sense of ourselves. Truly, Christ is far bigger than any of this. I made the statement above that the whole of the painting is greater than the sum of the parts. The fullness of reality is far too great for us to completely understand it or to piece it together like a puzzle or to add it up like a math equation. It is something we can only get glimpses of, but even these glimpses of the fullness of Christ allow us to become more and more the selves we are meant to be, in loving relationship with others and God, as we are meant to be.[1]

This is, of course, the ultimate goal, but to get there we must pay attention to each individual "strip." We must evaluate and question and ponder. You may have had a hunch, an inkling, that there was something missing, or fabricated, or clunky about your current worldview, while simultaneously knowing you are not completely wrong, either. The same is true for your friends and loved ones who have different views of the world than you. In the following chapters, we will examine what truth each of the worldviews holds, and we will think about the elements that have been added to fill in the gaps. We will find parts of each that are valuable and trustworthy: this is the original strip. We want to honor that core. We want to honor the truth revealed in each worldview. Examination will help us determine what has been added and what needs to be stripped away. In *Mere Christianity*, C. S. Lewis writes that we "do not have to believe that all the other religions are simply wrong all through. . . . All those religions, even the [strangest] ones, contain at least some hint of the truth."[2] Let us move forward in pursuit of those hints of truth and, ultimately, the fullness of reality.

CHAPTER 15

The Light of the World

The metaphor of the divided *Last Supper* painting has brought us to this point, but I recognize it won't help us to move *beyond* this point. The painting allows us to see the unity of truth—it allows us to cultivate a desire to see the masterpiece all together, to long for the unity of all truth—but we need a different metaphor or image to enable us to see the distinctions of the different parts of truth—the "strips" held by the different worldviews and the *consequences* of this division of truth.

Let us turn to thinking about truth as a chandelier.[1] Imagine a gigantic chandelier that at night can flood a huge cathedral with light. There are five brilliant lights in the chandelier, and each needs to be lit in order for the entire space to be filled with light. Four lights are around the outside, filling the north transept, the south transept, the nave, and the choir, and one is at the center filling the crossing, like a compass. Each light illuminates each section of this glorious and beautiful cathedral with its own light. If the light for one section is out, that section of the cathedral is dark. In this image, the center light is Jesus Christ, and Christ is also the light that emanates from each of the lights.[2] The only way that the entire cathedral can be fully seen is when all five of the lights are on, and the only way that the center light turns on is when all of the outside four lights are lit. Christ is the Light of the World, but we do not receive the benefit of the fullness of the Christ light unless we fully know who Christ is, represented by having all four of the other lights, the four parts of reality, on at the same time.

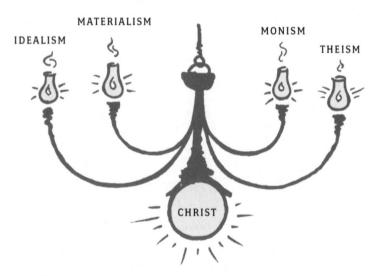

This new metaphor takes us beyond the painting metaphor in an important way: it highlights the necessity of working toward a complete worldview. A painting is essential to human- ity in a much different way than light is. Without light, we stumble around in the dark. Without light, we can't even *see* paintings. For this reason, a chandelier helps us see the consequences of having only part of the full truth. Hanging only one strip of a painting on our wall might strike us as a little odd, but it wouldn't be a major problem; it may not seriously affect us because we wouldn't know it wasn't complete. We wouldn't know what we were missing. G. K. Chesterton admits that in some respects all art is limited; the artist cannot fit all of reality into one painting. In other words, all art is only a "silly strip" of the world. If only one light out of the five on the chandelier is turned on, however, we would recognize the lack of light, especially in a massive cathedral in the dark of night. We would surely miss the other four. We would want them all on so we could see more fully and more clearly. This metaphor has particular significance in relation to the allegory of the cave. Think of how many of us have grown used to two or three lights being out. Some of us have never had more than one working bulb in our whole existence. Some of us did not even know there were other lights available to be turned on.

The chandelier image also helps us recognize that each of the worldviews does have light, truth, dignity, and honor. My atheist friends have light, as do my Buddhist, Hindu, Muslim, Jewish, and pantheist friends. With this approach to worldview, none of the perspectives is completely in the dark, and we can see truth lit up in each worldview.

If you are reading this and you say you have Jesus—whom I have already claimed to be the fullness of reality—please don't skip ahead; don't assume you don't need this. Each one of us has areas of both light and darkness in our views and perspectives. Even if you have Jesus, you will still have areas of darkness or shadow in your views of him and in your perspectives on reality, yourself, and others. Your personal understanding of Christ is not as big and full as the actual person of Christ, who encompasses all of reality and *is* the Light of the World.

Jesus wants us to grow in our understanding of him, and he provides the help for doing so. Plato told us we must leave the cave on our own volition and power, but this is nearly impossible for us because we are not capable of even seeing or recognizing that we are in a cave. We are not capable of recognizing our own areas of darkness, and we *all* have some areas of darkness. We are truly ignorant on some level, not knowing what we don't know, and this is the darkest kind of ignorance. In the fourth act of Shakespeare's *Twelfth Night*, Malvolio is locked in a dark room and is being questioned by the fool, Feste. Feste says to Malvolio, "There is no darkness but ignorance." Malvolio replies from the dark cell, "I say this house is as dark as ignorance, though ignorance were as dark as hell."[3] Jesus himself says, "The eye is the lamp of the body. If your eyes are healthy, your whole body will be full of light. But if your eyes are unhealthy, your whole body will be full of darkness. If then the light within you is darkness, how great is that darkness!" (Matthew 6:22-23, NIV). To catch some of the weight of what Jesus says, I encourage you to reread that verse and replace the word *eye* with *worldview*. Jesus knows the greatness of our darkness, and he, the very light of the world, was willing to enter our "cave." He is still willing to enter our cavernous hearts and minds and to shine into our individual darkness. He reveals light to us and then gently leads us out of the cave to where we can see his full light. He does for us what we are not capable of doing for ourselves.

I love that Jesus says the "eye" is the "lamp" of the body. He clearly illustrates the magnitude and importance of worldview for all who will see it. World*view* impacts everything, and our view of the world is best described in terms of light and darkness. Light is what ultimately allows us to see. Without light, we are essentially blind, even if we have twenty-twenty vision. Jesus directly states that if our worldview is limited or fractured, if our "eye is bad," our "whole body"—in other words, our whole life—will be full of darkness. The warning is frightening when fully understood, because the one who created the world, created light, and created eyes, minds, and hearts is referring to people like you and me being blind and living in darkness while thinking we have plenty of light.

In the following four chapters, we will examine each of the worldviews using the chandelier metaphor. We will look at what truth is lit up by each view and what truths are shadowed by "turning off" the other lights. As you read the following chapters, it may be helpful to ponder some of the chandelier visuals and grasp a picture of this metaphor in your mind. Each of the four outer lights represents a different worldview. Remember, when all four are lit, the center—who is Jesus Christ, "the Light of the World"—lights up as well. When only one of the four outer lights is turned on, then all the other lights are dark.

I want you to imagine yourself standing at night under that chandelier in a large, beautiful cathedral, a cathedral filled with things or people you want to see—beautiful artwork, magnificent stained glass, or beloved family members and friends, even the latest ideas, inventions, discoveries, or books from around the world. Imagine only one light is on. You can see the portion of the cathedral that is under that light—with all that this portion holds, but the areas under the unlit lights are shadowed and dark. Imagine the longing you would feel to see what is in the shadowy areas. You know what is in them is wonderful, but you cannot experience what is in the shadows unless all the lights are turned on.

May this longing propel you in your pursuit of truth. Truth is real, and it can be trusted. The journey from the wall of the cave into the light is often difficult and gradual; it takes time to adjust to greater light and to see what is revealed by it. But this journey is imperative—and it's worth it.

CHAPTER 16

Idealism: Lights On and Off

The [Buddhist] deity is like a giant who should have lost his leg or hand and be always seeking to find it; but the Christian power is like some giant who in a strange generosity should cut off his right hand, so that it might of its own accord shake hands with him.

G. K. CHESTERTON

The light of idealism makes it clear there is a spiritual reality and spiritual perfection. Something objective outside of what we can see with our human, physical eyes does exist. This is a great truth. Idealism tells us that all the hints we have that there is a reality beyond the physical realm are indeed pointing to something. There is a spiritual reality that is as real as what we can see with our eyes, touch with our fingers, taste with our tongues, smell with our noses, and hear with our ears. Idealism tells us we are incomplete as we are, and this answers the longings we have to be better, to be more, to be in good relationship with others. This helps us make sense of the pain and chaos of the world surrounding us, for idealism tells us a perfect spiritual world exists independent of the broken, hurting one we are currently experiencing. This is why so many people adhere to, are drawn to, or at least admire and respect so much of Buddhism. Idealism tells us we have these longings for more and for something better because in spiritual reality there is an absolute, an objective reality that determines what absolute truth and beauty and goodness are.

Again, humans have a natural inclination to admire real beauty and truth and goodness. Somewhere deep inside they know there is gradation and differentiation and even a real standard for these things. While we all have different tastes and perspectives, idealism reveals the reality that beauty, goodness, and truth are not arbitrary, based solely on individual or even societal norms; they are absolute, based on and decided by the one absolute, objective reality: the one perfect ideal, god. Idealism, therefore, has given human beings a standard outside themselves, an absolute standard, a rock-solid, eternal, unchanging standard. In this standard, idealism has also given all humans a goal: to be perfect and whole, to be like god, to even attempt union with god—to become one with the perfect, spiritual ideal. Much of idealism in the religious sphere will even point humanity toward the insight that if there is any spiritual truth, goodness, and beauty within us, it originates from the one source of truth, goodness, and beauty.

These are great truths, but idealism has built an entire reality on these truths alone, and this leaves us with questions and with some deep shadows. For example, in pure idealism (as seen in devout Buddhism and some aspects of Hinduism), the perfect ideal can be vague and impersonal; it ends up being abstract and static. It can be detached and without personality. There is little or no relationship with this ideal other than its being a conceptual goal to strive for, and idealism offers no personal or relational help from a perfect being in attaining this goal. The perfect spiritual ideal tends to be much more a *state of being* (like Buddhism's nirvana) rather than a being itself. Nirvana does not have eyes or ears or hands or a heart. The Oxford English Dictionary offers this definition for nirvana: "A transcendent state in which there is neither suffering, desire, nor sense of self, and the subject is released from the effects of karma and the cycle of death and rebirth. It represents the final goal of Buddhism." Hinduism would assert much of this as well.

This way of thinking has unfortunate consequences when it is followed all the way to its conclusion. If, spiritually speaking, this god is perfection and the ultimate eternal standard is spiritual perfection, then consequently humans will find themselves striving to not simply be *like* god, or subserviently dwell *alongside* god, or live *with* god in solidarity, but ultimately striving to *become* god. Hinduism, along with Buddhism, pulls from this truth, noting that if there is any goodness, truth, and beauty in a human, it is because "god is dwelling in me as me." This sounds like a powerful, beautiful perspective until we settle into the hollow understanding that if it is true, then there is no *me*! This is one of the main tenets of Buddhism and Hinduism: there is no self, no *me*; there is only god. Union with god is not like marriage, in which the two become one and yet paradoxically remain two; union with god is absorption into god, at the expense and detachment of self. One loses oneself in god—and thus ends up without a self. While that may sound great at first hearing, it means for pure idealists that there is no "other" for god to love. Thus, there is no real love, because love requires at least two—and in idealism, there is only one. This point always reminds me of a three-hour lunch I had with a devout Buddhist who concluded I was selfish for wanting to have and maintain a self.

Furthermore, honest humans know that humans cannot become perfect on their own, but this is what idealism sets in front of them all the same: an endless striving after an impossible goal. In much of idealist thought, each human, upon achieving perfection, is absorbed into the ideal and ceases to be an individual self. This also means the material world has no lasting value and is not real. It does not matter; it is merely a shadow of spiritual reality and is meant to be shed and left behind more and more—and, ultimately, left behind entirely—as spiritual perfection is attained. This train of thought is what leads so many Buddhists to the wholesale rejection of the material realm as pure shadow and even evil. Though some embrace this concept of spiritually becoming one with the ideal "one," it assuredly undercuts a basic human desire to be unique, to be a person, to retain a sense of self and a relationship with others beyond this material world. We all want to be the best version of ourselves, but in almost all cases, we want to still be *ourselves*. Idealism tells us we are not really real until we lose all sense of self and become one with the ideal spiritual one. Real life in idealism starts after death, but it is a life without any sense of individuality. The Buddha pointedly states, "Life is suffering," and this is a statement based upon the premise that life before death is an illusion, a shadow of life. It is not life at all. Idealism's lights are shining on a beautiful ideal, but it is a sterile ideal, separate and so far above us that we cannot touch it. This ideal reveals several things about us. First, that we have a desire and a need for an absolute, for a standard of goodness and beauty and truth that is separate from us but accessible to us; a standard not made by us; a standard that is not relative. Second, that we want to be like this ideal but still retain our spiritual and material identity. And third, that we are incapable of making ourselves perfect. If I need to make myself perfect, I would need to be perfect in order to perfectly do so. A perfect person is the only person who could perfectly make themselves perfect. I know I am not perfect, and therefore I will not be capable of making myself perfect perfectly. We need help, and deep down, beneath our pride and self-sufficiency, we *want* help.

C. S. Lewis writes,

> Now what was the sort of "hole" man had got himself
> into? He had tried to set up on his own, to behave as if
> he belonged to himself. In other words, fallen man is not
> simply an imperfect creature who needs improvement:
> he is a rebel who must lay down his arms. Laying down
> your arms, surrendering, saying you are sorry, realising
> that you have been on the wrong track and getting ready
> to start life over again from the ground floor—that is the
> only way out of a "hole." This process of surrender . . . is
> what Christians call repentance. . . . And here comes the
> catch. Only a bad person needs to repent: only a good
> person can repent perfectly. The worse you are the more

you need it and the less you can do it. The only person
who could do it perfectly would be a perfect person—
and he would not need it.[1]

Take a few moments right now. Close your eyes, and practice thinking of perfect ideas. Earlier we thought of cars and
chairs. Try thinking of the perfect version of *anything*. It is easy
to come to the conclusion that nothing on earth is perfect or
permanent. The bright light of idealism shines on us in this
moment. Remember the exercise from chapter 8, where I asked
you to think of the perfect being? No flaws, perfectly true, perfectly beautiful, perfectly honest, perfectly moral, perfectly
powerful, filled with vigor and life, perfectly good, perfectly
generous, perfectly loving, with a perfect history and legacy . . .
Take some time to ponder on this being again. Were you thinking of yourself? Again, I have never had anyone say yes—and
mean it. This, in essence, is the piercing light of idealism. We
are all, on some level, idealists at this point. We recognize that
we ourselves are not perfect.

Keep in mind that in order to be that imagined perfect
being, you would by necessity have to stop being yourself as
you are right now—because you just admitted that you are not
that being. Additionally, in idealism, there is only *one* perfect
being—rather, one perfect *state* of being—and all others are
subject to that one. The goal in idealism is to figure out which
one is the real one and then strive to attain unity with that
one. Even if you were to name Jesus Christ as your perfect
being—a great answer—I remind you that while you may have
been taught to be *like* Jesus, the Bible does not tell us to let go
of ourselves and *become* Jesus. The apostle Paul writes, "You

should imitate me, just as I imitate Christ" (1 Corinthians 11:1). Again, we *imitate*, not *become*. We are told in Scripture that Jesus wants a relationship with us, that Jesus is, in essence, our older brother in the family of God the Father. Jesus was fully, materially, and spiritually alive and himself when he lived as God in the flesh, filled with God's Holy Spirit. I, too, need to be fully me, with my own individual spirit, yet with God's Spirit also fully in me. I am not only to be filled with God's Holy Spirit, as Jesus was, but also to be fully me, not God. This is only possible with the spiritual and physical distinction revealed by the light of theism, with the spiritual unity revealed by the light of monism, and with the physicality revealed by the hard, solid light of materialism.

In turning off the light and the distinctions found in theism, an idealist turns off the opportunity for there to be a real, autonomous "self" in loving relationship with a real and distinct "Creator" of that self. In turning off the physical light of materialism, the idealist turns off the bodily presence of real selves that matter here and now and that are individual and unique. In turning off the unifying light of monism, an idealist has turned off what allows the spiritual and material to be united and connected in eternal, sustaining, life-giving unity.

In the third chapter of his famous letter to the church in Rome, the apostle Paul states, "Everyone has sinned; we all fall short of God's glorious standard" (Romans 3:23). This is much of the essence of what is meant when an idealist admits he or she is not perfect. Furthermore, what is this sentence essentially saying in the light of idealism? In idealism, the onus for attaining perfect unity with the spiritual ideal lies in the shadowy image of that ideal. It is like a picture of a person trying to attain actual existence *as* that person. The picture hopes, through perpetual striving and hard work, to become one with the living person. This is an impossible task: for a lifeless, two-dimensional object to make itself three-dimensional and then give itself life. In Christ-centered theism, the Good News of the gospel is that God so loved us, his unique creation made in his image, that he chose to make those who have become imperfect *perfect*—individually and uniquely perfect! Paul continues in the following verse, "Yet God, in his grace, freely makes us right in his sight. He did this through Christ Jesus when he freed us from the penalty for our sins" (Romans 3:24). In a free, gracious act of love, God offers this to all the imperfect images because we must be perfect in order to dwell in loving relationship with the God who is perfect. (By nature, a being who is perfect has perfect standards; therefore, our perfection is required in order for us to be in relationship with the God who is perfectly perfect in and of himself.)

In the third chapter of the Gospel of John, Jesus says God does this because he loves the world. Furthermore, Jesus says there is no striving or work required to attain this necessary perfection (*righteousness* is the biblical term). For good reason, John 3:16 is a very popular verse in a fascinating, poetic book about God. It says this: "God so loved the world that he gave his one and only Son, that whoever believes in him shall not perish but have eternal life" (NIV). It's an amazing statement, but it is the sentences that come just before it that intrigue me even more in a context such as idealism. So let's look at the scene in which this statement is set.

Jesus is speaking with a very religious man named Nicodemus. Jesus, as a good teacher, knows he needs to give

Nicodemus a point of reference or comparison for this gift of salvation. Ironically, Nicodemus is what we might call a religious theistic idealist: he is part of a Jewish sect called the Pharisees, and Pharisees were known for their strict observance of God's law. For most of his life, Nicodemus has been caught up in trying to make himself morally and religiously perfect in order to please God. Nicodemus is unaware he is speaking with God in the flesh, who is lovingly and relationally offering him the Good News of righteousness and perfection, attained by grace, not through striving and personal works of sacrifice and purity. Before Jesus makes the incredible offer of salvation in John 3:16, he sets the stage.

Now, you need to understand that both Jesus and Nicodemus have incredible knowledge of the Old Testament—they've memorized it! Jesus could have picked anything in the Old Testament to compare salvation to: he could have referred to the parting of the Red Sea, the blood on the doorposts in Egypt, the ram sacrificed for Isaac, the falling of the walls of Jericho, the fire from heaven with Elijah. Rather than any of these, Jesus picks the story of the snake on a pole. Here is what he says:

> Just as Moses lifted up the snake in the wilderness, so the Son of Man must be lifted up, that everyone who believes may have eternal life in him.
>
> For God so loved the world that he gave his one and only Son, that whoever believes in him shall not perish but have eternal life. For God did not send his Son into the world to condemn the world, but to save the world through him.
>
> JOHN 3:14-17, NIV

The snake-on-a-pole incident is told in Numbers 21. The Israelites were being bitten by poisonous snakes in the wilderness (they were not yet in the Promised Land.) The people were dying from these snakebites and needed to be saved from them. They asked Moses to plead with God on their behalf. Rather than God eradicating all the snakes (which makes logical sense to me), God told Moses to fashion a bronze snake and put it on a pole. Whoever looked at the snake on the pole would be saved from the deadly snakebites. Salvation from death was accomplished by a simple glance.

We, too, are poisoned. The poison of imperfection and sin is all around us and in us, coursing through our communities and our bloodstreams. According to Jesus, salvation from this toxic situation is a glance at the Fullness of Reality giving himself up to restore us to our full selves and to a loving relationship with him. Jesus tells Nicodemus that salvation is a glance, not a long striving of self-righteousness. It is righteousness (perfection) offered as a gift; it is salvation through meaningful, trusting, hopeful eye contact with the living God—who was sitting right in front of him! I wonder if their eyes met in the starlight in that moment.

If Nicodemus had been a Buddhist, meeting Jesus on another rooftop in another conversation, he would have had to consider this teacher's profound message. The invitation here is not to let go of self and attain perfect union with God *as* God through suffering and striving. Jesus' invitation is to retain and become oneself by *ceasing* to strive, by *receiving* the gift of perfection—becoming the perfected version of yourself in a loving relationship, as yourself, with God. The eightfold path of the Buddha and the path of loving grace offered by Jesus

Christ are two very different paths built from two very different trust lists. Remember Elisha's servant, afraid of the physical army surrounding the city? When his eyes were opened to the reality of the far greater spiritual army, he no longer feared. The perception of reality he chose to trust did not change the reality, but it certainly affected him! In the same way, the perception of reality *you* choose to trust will not change the truth of Prime Reality. But it will change your understanding of reality and your daily decisions within reality. When the light of Christ is turned off in your trust list, authentic, life-giving, divine love and grace are left powerless as an influence in your life.

CHAPTER 17

Materialism:
Lights On and Off

As an explanation of the world, materialism has a sort of insane
simplicity.... We have at once the sense of it covering everything and
the sense of it leaving everything out.... [The materialist] understands
everything, and everything does not seem worth understanding.
His cosmos may be complete in every rivet and cog-wheel, but still
his cosmos is smaller than our world. Somehow his scheme ... is not
thinking of the real things of the earth, of fighting peoples or proud
mothers, or first love or fear upon the sea. The earth is so very large,
and the cosmos is so very small.

G. K. CHESTERTON

In the light of materialism, the physical world is valued and
honored. Actions done in the physical world have effect; the
consequences can be seen and felt and observed. This is an
important revelation, for it gives importance to what we experience through our senses. The beauty and goodness of what
is seen, touched, tasted, smelled, and heard is real and true.
Our lives matter here and now. The *now* matters. Material preferences matter. *Matter* matters. As my friend Bishop Stewart
Ruch says, "If I like my coffee with cream and sugar and you
like yours black, both are valid choices, and our individuality
can be celebrated." Much of life is relative and simply based on

preference, like the smell of roses and the flavor of ice cream. When we hold someone's hand, see someone's smile, hear the sound of a loved one's voice, or taste a delicious meal, we have experienced something real. Furthermore, our perception of and desire for material distinctions are significant and important because they reveal the desire for autonomy and individuality. The earth, with all its ever-transforming, varied beauty, should be cared for and honored. The creative, unique makeup of each material thing, both organic and inorganic, is to be celebrated as the epitome of existential reality.

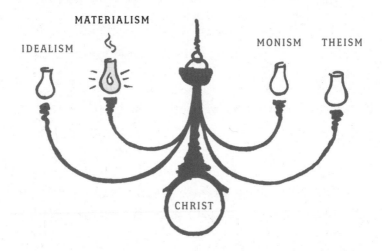

And this is where the shadow of materialism begins, for if matter is all that matters and nothing outside the material world exists or matters, this has huge ramifications. Feelings and emotions then are nothing more than chemical reactions, as are rational thoughts, intellectual assertions, or personal opinions. The longings we have for relationship and unity and connection are not actually real beyond chemical bonds and electrical impulses, and there can be no such thing as authentic free will (and, therefore, no true sense of autonomy and moral responsibility). All that is "real" will be the physical interactions caused by chemical reactions, firing randomly and yet semipredictably, but totally outside of human control.

As this book is being penned, humanity is on the brink of creating self-piloting cars and aircraft. In the foreseeable future, a car could drive itself without a "self" inside it. The vehicle would be propelled by an internal (yet dependent) energy source; it would completely react to input and output of information received and transmitted through sensors; and this information would be processed through a brain of sorts, a computer that reacts to the environment and makes predetermined choices based on preset learned or stored information. The device will appear to be making choices, will look as if it is deciding what to do next. However, people who know how these devices work would adamantly argue that the device is not truly choosing anything freely; it cannot go beyond what its program allows. If a child runs in front of the car, it will stop simply because it has been programmed to stop when anything gets in its path. The car itself has made no moral decision in the process.

Even if artificial intelligence gets to the point where it is making decisions that appear to be self-directed and autonomous, without a nonmaterial soul connected to it, artificial intelligence (with an emphasis on the word *artificial*) will never actually be able to make real choices. In short, it is not actually "choosing." What appear to be real choices are simply lightning-fast reactions to stimuli in in the immediate environment combined with stored information contained in and connected to a global memory network.

For someone who only trusts in the material realm as really real and believes all we are is an amalgamation of electrons and matter, we are no different in our essence from a computer or battery-operated toy. All that is different is the stuff we are made of and the complexity of the device. Therefore, there is no sense of freedom or control. It takes a being within the shell of the car or airplane, in connection with the device and with the ability to have some sense of control over the device, for there to be any real essence of freedom and choice related to the driver or pilot and the car or plane. Theists refer to this pilot/driver as the soul or spirit of a person. It is the nonmaterial driver of the body; it is in connection with the body but is not the body (as seen at death). For a theist, the human soul is individual and unique. Each body is connected to a soul, but the soul is not limited to the substance of the body.

Smarter people than I have written plenty on this issue. I simply offer an illustration of what the idea of the human soul can mean when we view it in the lights of both monism and theism: if each human has a unique soul in connection with a particular body, and if each human invites the unifying Spirit of God to indwell his or her body to live in relation with, *not as*, that human soul in that particular body, the ramifications are incredible. The presence of two souls inside the physical finiteness of a body allows for individuality, uniqueness, connectedness, unity, distinction, autonomy, love, and freedom! It allows for the stuff of real, meaningful life. When the lights of theism and monism and the spiritual are turned off, however, real living—real life!—is turned off. We are simply left with chemical reactions and the appearance of life.

If you take the idea of complete materialism to its ultimate end, life becomes meaningless and loses its purpose. An authentic atheist will wholeheartedly embrace this concept; interestingly, though, few are authentic in their understanding of the natural consequences of trusting materialism. Here are a few of these consequences: what we think of as our "self" ceases to exist when the heart stops beating and the chemical reactions stop firing. Reality is restricted to the material world, and this material world holds no inherent sense of any real, objective standard of right and wrong; it can't because there is nothing other than the material to allow for any real objectivity. Morality has, therefore, no real meaning. Right and wrong, beauty and goodness, truth and honor are nothing more than concepts, determined by individuals or groups of individuals and their existential perspective on reality. If materialism is the whole truth, good and evil are arbitrary; there is no set standard, no objectivity. This means that, although there can be preferences, there can be no evil and no good.

To illustrate this with my students, I ask them each to draw an inch on a piece of paper. "Who has the right inch?" I ask. Without a ruler, can we determine that? Do we simply pick one student's "inch" and use that as the standard until another student argues forcefully and skillfully enough that their inch is better? Until we pull out a ruler with its determined, absolute, authoritative, objective inch, any "inch" we draw is arbitrary. Of course, any materialist who claims a sense of objectivity for morality will do it on these premises. They will assert that humanity has all agreed on our "inch," or better yet, that our genes have decided what works best to perpetuate the genome. It is rare to find a modern materialist who will clearly articulate the actual absurdity of modern human morality for the materialist trust list. Albert Camus in his work *The Stranger* and Friedrich Nietzsche in *Thus Spake Zarathustra* were at least honest and open about this natural consequence of killing an objective authority for morality. Objective, authentic meaning and morality die when God dies. I do not have any issues with Nietzsche when he states that God died—I believe that happened two thousand years ago on the cross at Calvary just outside Jerusalem. Nietzsche's real stab at theism occurs when he states that "God remains dead."

This point can be further illustrated by the late atheist Christopher Hitchens's bestseller *God Is Not Great: How Religion Poisons Everything.* I had already encountered the trust list of the famous Oxford atheist Richard Dawkins (after filling his pockets by purchasing three of his books and thoroughly unpacking his devoted trust in probability, the scientific method of observation and theorizing, and the unlimited potential of infinite time). While I appreciated Dawkins's honesty—at least in the title of chapter 4 of his book *The God Delusion*, "Why There Almost Certainly Is No God"—I was a bit disappointed at his inauthenticity in not mentioning the natural consequences of his beliefs, such as the absurdity of life without meaning, morality, autonomy, and free will. So when several people told me that Hitchens's book was quite compelling, I had high hopes that it would answer some of the questions I'd had after reading Dawkins's works.

I loved reading *God Is Not Great.* It was life transforming for me as a Christian. Hitchens is an intriguing writer who crafts arguments with energy and vigor. He does a smashing job talking about the atrocities and abuses of religion. I found myself cheering out loud in angry solidarity while reading his excellent description of the horrors of slavery, the perpetual abuses of women in the name of God, the pettiness of denominational divisiveness over rituals, and the devious exploitation of the farcical miraculous (his choice of the word *tawdry* is brilliant). On top of all this, I simply love the yellow cover and the audacity of the title. It is compelling . . . but unfortunately inaccurate.

I wanted to use the book in my class but knew the title would get in the way, and I wasn't sure what to do about that. I had just finished Hitchens's book, and I was still thinking about it. Then it hit me: I knew how I could use the book in my class. I grabbed my copy of the book and a Sharpie marker. It all became perfectly clear when I retitled the book. It was the same message Nietzsche had sent the world so many years before. My new cover read, "God's Followers Are Not That Great: How the Abuse of Religion Poisons Everything." Like a dislocated shoulder put back into place, the whole of the book now made sense. I had a new friend in Christopher Hitchens.

He had not really written about religion or God; he had written about how the misguided, ego-driven, selfish, narcissistic, shortsighted, dim-witted followers of God, like me, have at times misrepresented the true God and how we so-called devotees have misused and abused religion in God's name. Hitchens did not write about how grace and love poison everything. He did not write about the toxic abuse of forgiveness and mercy. He did not write about how loving, authentic, healthy, life-changing, and life-giving supernatural signs, wonders, miracles, and encounters with the relational and personal God have ruined and destroyed the individuals who truly experienced them. He did not write about a loving God who saves the world at his own expense and then offers salvation as a free gift to all of humanity. Nor did he write about how this God desires deep, beautiful harmony and mutual honor among all people and his amazing creation. He did not write about a God who "delight[s]" in us, who "rejoice[s] over [us] with joyful songs" (Zephaniah 3:17). Nor did he do justice to the compassionate, generous, and powerful character and nature of Jesus as found in the Gospels.

I quickly wrote a letter to Hitchens. I wanted to know if he had published any materialist writing on the absurdity of life, the capricious nature of life without free will, and the absurdity of morality. In the letter, I mentioned my frustration on this matter.

The tension I felt compelled to address with Mr. Hitchens was his glaring lack of acknowledgment of the horrors of authentic materialistic morality. He did a great job of pointing out the abuses of religion—for which I applaud him. But he is only able to do this because of the overt and obvious standards for morality that "religion" has—many of which he agrees with. He opposes slavery because of his desire to champion freedom of the human will, which is ironic because authentic atheism adheres to the notion that humans do not even have a will, let alone a free one, as Sam Harris finally admitted in one of his latest books on atheism.[1] Hitchens ridicules fake miracles, not realizing his argument is ridiculous, that the very word *fake* implies there must be something real to be counterfeited: truth is necessary for a lie to exist. Hitchens talks about how immoral patriarchal, domineering religion can be in its abuses toward women—and yet neglects to address the standard the God of the Hebrew Bible himself set by making women of equal value to men as equally made in the image of God. Women thus are to be treated with the same honor as men as half of the representation of the nature of God to all of humanity. He also failed to address that true atheism has no objective standard to honor or value women, and I am left to wonder about the foundation on which he bases his authority for the humane treatment of any human.

Finally and most important, Hitchens rails about the abuses of morality in religion with all of the bullying, terrorism, torture, and even killing that at times happens. Admittedly, humans, using the name of God, have committed some of the most unspeakably horrific atrocities ever committed on this planet. And that is my main point: Hitchens can only call these actions horrifying and abusive if there is a real standard, and the very religions he despises provide the standard. I call terrorism an abuse of religion because there is a standard set by God to love and forgive my enemies, not terrorize and torture them. Jesus even says I am not supposed to hate my enemies simply because of what it does to my heart. When Hitchens sees terrorist activities, he notices something is inherently wrong only because there is a God-given objective standard (which exists even if he does not acknowledge it), and Hitchens recognizes that terrorism is a deviation from it.

My question for Hitchens was whether he had considered the potential horrors of atheistic, unobjective morality. What would we do in a world in which there is no objective standard for morality? We would usher in a world with no abuses of morality because there would be no standard to abuse or from which to deviate. If Hitchens got his way and religions were dismantled, thus removing their standards for morality, then he would essentially have no right to be upset about crimes against his personal preferences of morality. I am more concerned about a world in which nothing can be an abuse of morality because there is no acknowledged real and truly objective standard of morality than I am about a world where we can all point out the glaring abuses of morality based on the natural law of morality that God has embedded in each of us, hidden in the created order, and even shared with humans in the special revelation of his Word.

C. S. Lewis has some very insightful commentary on this issue. It is helpful to keep in mind that Lewis was a staunch atheist for more than fifteen years of his adult life before he accepted Christianity. He says,

> If a good God made the world, why has it gone wrong? . . .
>
> My argument against God was that the universe seemed so cruel and unjust. But how had I got this idea of *just* and *unjust*? A man does not call a line crooked unless he has some idea of a straight line. . . .
>
> Atheism turns out to be too simple. If the whole universe has no meaning, we should never have found out that it has no meaning: just as, if there were no light in the universe and therefore no creatures with eyes, we should never know it was dark.[2]

The light of materialism gives value to the physical world. It declares it real. This is a truth to hold on to while we acknowledge that many other answers presented by materialism are shadowy, insubstantial, and do not adequately answer the deep questions of the human heart. If you follow materialism far enough, in fact, the shadows of materialism ironically begin to negate even the light it reveals, for we want life and relationships to hold meaning and purpose; we want love to be real; we want humans to be held accountable for their choices; we want to be able to say gross injustice—actions such as rape and murder and child abuse—is wrong and evil; many of us want to believe there is a spirit within us that continues after physical death. Every human I have ever met has agreed that we all have a sense of justice deep within us that makes us desire all to be well for all people, yet all of this becomes absurd when we turn off the lights of the other worldviews.

⁜ o **CHAPTER 18**

Monism:
Lights On and Off ⁚ ⁜

Pantheists usually believe that God . . . animates the universe as you animate your body: that the universe almost *is* God, so that if it did not exist He would not exist either, and anything you find in the universe is a part of God. . . . If you do not take the distinction between good and bad very seriously, then it is easy to say that anything you find in this world is a part of God. But, of course, if you think some things really bad, and God really good, then you cannot talk like that. You must believe that God is separate from the world and that some of the things we see in it are contrary to His will.

C. S. LEWIS

Pure monists say we are all united and connected, and quite frankly this is true: the entire universe is connected materially (molecularly and through light) and even supernaturally/spiritually through the Holy Spirit of Christ. On some level, this should not surprise Christians. Jesus and Paul clearly say that it is Christ that *unites* us (see John 17:1-5, 13-26; Romans 6:5; 1 Corinthians 1:10) and that Christ created *all things* and holds *all creation* together (see Colossians 1:11-22). This means all humanity is far more connected than it is divided; humans are connected with each other, just as they are connected with nature and animals. The bright light of monism offers a beacon of hope and motivation to seek unity and harmony with all of life—with all of reality! All, together—both the material and the spiritual—make up reality, and all are somehow mysteriously connected.[1] Monism values both the material and spiritual worlds by saying they are one, a unified whole manifesting itself in two different ways. Reality is like a person with both a front and a back. The front of a person may look entirely unlike his or her back, but this person is still only one human; both sides work together making the whole person. Reality, therefore, can be found in both the physical, material world and the mysterious, spiritual world. Both have meaning; both have purpose. There is a connection to be pursued, and it can and should be pursued through physical reality as well as through spiritual reality, for the two are not separate but united. One affects the other. They are connected to each other like a coin with two sides. Spirituality is embedded in the material reality, thus making beauty possible. Material reality is embedded in spirituality, thus giving spirituality expression and shape. Matter matters. Spiritual reality matters. Everything matters. Thoughts and actions completed in the material world affect the spiritual world and vice versa.

But this light by itself leads directly to the shadows. For if the entirety of everything—together, connected and united—is "god," then, like in pure materialism, there is no objective absolute standard, nor can there be an objective absolute standard that determines good or evil, truth or falsity. Being united "*in* Christ" is categorically different from being united "*as* Christ." As mentioned earlier, materialism and idealism can and should be considered monistic in that there is the belief in only one reality as Prime Reality; thus, there is no option for the "other" to exist to create any objectivity, relationship, or value. Similarly, if everything is god, then we have, in effect, lost god. God loses identity, and humans lose theirs as well. Having the Holy Spirit of Christ in you, with you, is not the same as having God's Spirit in you, *as* you. When humans cease to have a unique, definitive self, there is no basis for relationship; we are all part of a waterlogged watercolor painting that never takes shape, that has no one painting it—at least no one outside the painting.

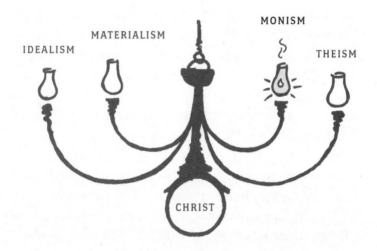

Rather, everything in the painting *is* the painting.

In pure monism, purpose is lost; distinction is lost; relationship is lost; right and wrong are lost. The Star Wars movies are good examples of this. I still love the Star Wars movies—I believe all great stories point us to the true, great story we are in, and these are great stories! However, I am aware that when we watch Star Wars, we impose our view of morality on it; the Jedi are the "good guys," and Darth Vader and the Empire are the "bad guys." But there is nothing objective, no overarching authoritative being or ideal standard in the movie's monistic viewpoint that determines this. The Force, in everything and in everyone, is amoral. It makes no distinctions and sets no standards and has no ultimate purpose. Viewers often see Anakin's turn away from the Jedi and toward the dark side as a choice for evil, but the movie does not necessarily present it that way. It is merely a choice of preference.

I remember watching the scene in *Revenge of the Sith* when Anakin is confronted by Obi-Wan Kenobi about his choice of loyalty. When Anakin is cautioned that he is turning from good toward evil, he argues that he simply sees it differently. "From my point of view," he says, "the Jedi are evil."[2] I jumped up and danced around the room at this point, exclaiming, "He actually says it out loud!" My nephew laughed, yet we later talked about how, in the context of the universe and worldview of Star Wars, Anakin—or any character—is free to make that choice. There is no ultimate consequence, for the Force may be powerful, but it is not concerned with right and wrong, only perspective.

You may be wondering right now, *If both worldviews result in having no objective standard for morality, what's the difference between materialism and monism?* It's a good question. The distinction lies in the belief in spiritual power. Monism holds that humans are both material and spiritual beings, but monism, like materialism, holds no human ultimately accountable for the choices he or she makes. In both views, humans are free to make whatever "choices" suit them best. (And for both, ironically, this so-called "choice" is merely the perception of choice, since there is no real self-direction in either of these worldviews.) Since there is no god to submit to, with a will that determines good and evil, then each human's will is, essentially, the will of god. The end results—as seen in lives lived completely by monistic or materialistic principles—seem very similar.

G. K. Chesterton comments on the need for an objective, absolute standard in *Orthodoxy*:

> I agree . . . that there is an authoritative need to believe the things that are necessary to the human mind. But I say that one of those necessities precisely is a belief in objective truth. The pragmatist tells a man to think what he must think and never mind the Absolute. But precisely one of the things that he must think is the Absolute. This philosophy, indeed, is a kind of verbal paradox. Pragmatism is a matter of human needs; and one of the first of human needs is to be something more than a pragmatist. . . .
>
> It is vain for eloquent atheists to talk of the great truths that will be revealed if once we see free thought begin. We have seen it end. It has no more questions to ask; it has questioned itself. You cannot call up any wilder vision than a city in which men ask themselves if they have any selves. You cannot fancy a more skeptical world than that in which men doubt if there is a world. . . . We have no more questions left to ask. We have looked for questions in the darkest corners and on the wildest peaks. We have found all the questions that can be found. It is time we gave up looking for questions and began looking for answers.[3]

And that is what we will do in the conclusion of this book.

CHAPTER 19

Religious Theism: Lights On and Off

Acts in God's eye what in God's eye he is—
Christ—for Christ plays in ten thousand places,
Lovely in limbs, and lovely in eyes not his
To the Father through the features of men's faces.

GERARD MANLEY HOPKINS

Now we come to religious theism, the worldview that includes, but is not limited to, the religions of Islam, Judaism, Christianity, and tribal religions that worship a creator and the Great Spirit. I have made my view of Christ very clear by this point, so I understand readers may assume I will see more light in this worldview than in the others. After all, I clearly am not approaching this study as a materialist or monist or idealist, so my view of "light" and "dark" will be biased from a theistic perspective. However, it is my contention that Christ himself is the fullness of reality, so I see lights on and lights off in this worldview as well. For this chapter, I will stay focused on the broader philosophical boundaries of theism in general and save the key distinctions between religions for later.

Shining in the light of religious theism is the idea that there is a perfect ideal being: God. As in idealism, God is complete goodness, truth, and beauty; therefore, God is the standard. All attempts at goodness, beauty, and truth are measured against God, and this standard draws a clear line between good and evil. The God of religious theism, though, is a creator, a creator who created both spiritual and material reality. Both are real; both are valued. This truth is much like what is revealed in monism, but there is a very important difference: the created spiritual and material realities are distinct from God. This light illuminates the deep feeling we humans have that there is a right way to act and a wrong way—and this "way" comes from outside us. C. S. Lewis puts it like this: humans "have this curious idea that they ought to behave in a certain way, and cannot really get rid of it," and this leads to the idea that there is "something which is directing the universe, and which appears in [them] as a law urging [them] to do right and making [them] responsible and uncomfortable when [they] do wrong."[1] Religious theism sheds light on these ideas held deep within us. This, too, is similar to what is revealed by the light of idealism, but the unique light of religious theism illuminates the distinction of God from creation as not just a creator but a relational being. The goal for humanity is still to actualize our true selves, essentially to become perfect, to become like God, but in religious theism, humans do not become God or even a part of God. They remain unique and individual, with both material and spiritual "sides" of their being, and God remains God. The God of religious theism is not indistinct and vague but has personality and being. Furthermore, as God's creation, we humans have a standard and a purpose: to live up to God's perfect standard, to be in good relationship with God and other humans.

As I pointed out in chapter 11, the most important aspect of the philosophy of theism is represented in the painting of the *Creation of Adam* in the Sistine Chapel. Adam and God are positioned a short distance from each other, and each has one hand outstretched toward the other, but they are not quite touching. God's pointer finger is extended as if Adam has just sprung forth from it. I know that brilliant art historians and critics could go on for pages about the meaning embedded within that painting, but my focus here is the relationship potential, the "space" between Adam's and God's fingers, and the fact that Adam and God look very similar—God is presented as a being like Adam. Adam is in the image of God; Adam is remarkably "like God," and conversely, God is "like Adam"—like us. Consider the profundity of the statement from the Bible: "In the image of God he created them; male and female he created them" (Genesis 1:27). If Adam and Eve are in the image of God, then God is at least on some level represented in the image of Adam and Eve. Otherwise, humanity's creation in the image of God would not be a true statement. The value of being in the image of God and being *like* God but *not* God and of being *like* other humans but *not* other humans is that we all exist distinct from each other enough to not be each other. This distinction is what allows for relationship and free will. Free will and relationship offer purpose, meaning, and value to human existence.

As mentioned earlier, all the other worldviews are monistic in essence; theism is the only worldview with a trust in the distinct "otherness" of beings, which allows for true "I"-"Thou" relationships. Without this distinction of theism—that "space" between the fingers in the Sistine Chapel—we lose our distinction and diversity and simply become extensions of God, like marionettes or extra appendages; we lose our selves and slip into the one "self" of God. Thus, theism is the only worldview in which relationship, free will, love, and value can actually exist with any real meaning. Yet this alone is not enough. Without the truth and light of monism, humans would be literally *distinct* from each other and God—actually separated from God, who is the author and sustainer of life, particularly eternal life.

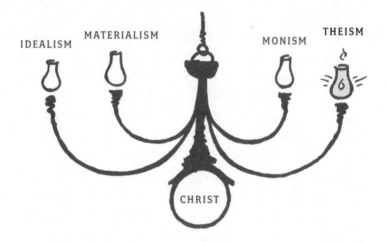

Just as in the other worldviews, the light turned off in theism is in many ways related to the light turned on. The understanding of God, and of God's objective morality, can make religious theism either hellish or beautiful. Without the light of idealism, religious theism does not need to have love and goodness at the core of its objective morality. Without love and goodness, religious theism is abusive and controlling, even terrifying. Though we have that "curious idea" of right and wrong deep within us, without a concrete, accurate definition (theology) or picture or image of God, our view of right and wrong—and therefore of God—can be terribly skewed. We can create our own individual god, who approves what we approve, likes who and what we like, and dislikes who and what we dislike. Then, we can religiously use godlike authority to condone or condemn others based on our version of "God's" standard for behavior and even value. This hellish abuse is what compels authors like Christopher Hitchens to write books about the "poison" of religion. Without the light of unity (shed powerfully and profoundly by monism), religious theism creates us-versus-them attitudes that over-celebrate distinction and differences, that use rules and moralism to intentionally exclude and create an "in" crowd and an "out" one. In Christianity alone, this has produced thousands upon thousands of religious denominations—and this is the faith that claims to follow Christ, who prayed that his followers would be one (see John 17:21). Islam and Judaism have similar divisive denominational issues.

Without the idea of unity, religious theists are free to create a god who is not concerned with the good of all people, with the good of all creation. For many religious theists, their god does not have to be the god *of all*; he can simply be a god who is for one particular group, who is against all others. Without the essential light of materialism, the god created by religious theism need not be concerned with the here and now and the physical state of people and the world. Religious theism unlit by materialism is free to focus only on a later existence in a spiritual realm. It can justify this focus and treat it as if it is more important than the material. People who follow this kind of spiritually focused theism tend to think that the most important thing—perhaps even the only thing—is getting to heaven and saving souls for heaven. Often Christians with this worldview forget or have not heard or don't believe that God came to earth and dwelled in a material body because if God dons a body, the material realm is valuable. They may even have prayed the Lord's Prayer and found themselves asking for God's Kingdom to come on earth, just as it is in heaven, yet all the while have never taken that statement seriously. According to Jesus, earth (and therefore the material realm) matters to Father God. The shepherd David writes in Psalm 19 that creation, the material realm, proclaims the glory of God and speaks about it every day!

Without the other three lights, religious theism tends to create a god who is perhaps the "ideal" for a particular individual or group but who is not the ideal for all, who is not complete, absolute, untainted truth, beauty, and goodness. I will now speak for Christians and not necessarily the other theistic religions. It can be easy to forget that "God so loved the world" (John 3:16, NIV). It can be easy to forget that Christ's birth was announced as "good news . . . to *all* people" (Luke 2:10, emphasis added). I will now speak for all theistic religions and not necessarily just Christians. When religious theism is taken to the extreme, particularly related to the truth of distinction and personal autonomy, it has, essentially, set aside the true God, created a human concept of a god controlled by a religion, established a rigid moral code, and embossed the entire system with the stamp of religious authority, a powerful stamp indeed.[2]

If you picked up this book as a religious theist, be it as a follower of Islam, Judaism, a tribal religion, or Christianity, you must ask yourself where you have potentially turned off the lights of the truths held by idealism, materialism, and monism. In what ways have you or your ism created a false god and a misuse of religion and religious authority?

CHAPTER 20

The Power of Paradox

This was the big fact about Christian ethics; the discovery of the new balance. Paganism had been like a pillar of marble, upright because proportioned with symmetry. Christianity was like a huge and ragged and romantic rock, which, though it sways on its pedestal at a touch, yet, because its exaggerated excrescences exactly balance each other, is enthroned there for a thousand years.

G. K. CHESTERTON

It is human default to deny the lights of any worldview other than our own. We are, in many ways, more comfortable living in the shadows, where we assume we have all the light there is. Many of us have never been directly invited to consider that more light is available to us. But when we become aware that there is more light, when sparks of that light are revealed to us, we are faced with a decision: Do we begin the arduous and often painful journey toward the light, or do we simply stay put?

This journey into the full light can be long and is sometimes almost cyclical—we feel as if we are learning the same "lessons" again and again, but each time around, there is a greater fullness and depth to what we learn and experience. Many teachers, philosophers, and writers are starting to use a helix as an effective metaphor for this concept because a helix is linear and cyclical at the same time. This journey will never allow us to feel as if we have arrived. We will always be learning, always be growing, always be stepping into a little more light. I often liken this worldview journey to a Shakespearean play, for in a sense the story does not end when the curtain drops. Shakespeare's stories and characters are so close to real-life stories and real-life characters that we understand the play represents a slice of the story of life; the characters represent you, me, us. People continue on with their lives after one story is finished; they embark on new stories that are also continuations of their old stories, that are part of their overall stories, that are part of the eternal love story already written and still being written by God.

If this is what you choose, to open your eyes and ears and heart to the great adventure story, to become a pilgrim on an ever-brightening journey to a holy place, you must embrace the idea of paradox, for reality is paradoxical. It is both material and spiritual; it is united but distinct; it is objective yet relative; and it is brutally impersonal and intimately personal.

This is the power of paradox. This is the truth and power of mystery. All worldviews, religions, isms, and ways have at their cores a deep sense of mystery and wonder. If you continue to press into them and ask questions of them, all of them (even materialism) will lead you to a place of paradox, and if you enter fully into this place of paradox, you are forced to surrender your belief that you have everything figured out, that you have all the answers. And this place of surrender and acceptance is a good place; it's a place where you can begin to look for truth.

G. K. Chesterton knew this. He implies that the power of paradox is what unlocked the truth and freedom of Christianity for him. I know many people will say paradox is a wimpy alternative to seeking "real truth." They often tell me I am just giving up my quest for true understanding, accepting mystery when a resolution is possible. But I believe paradox is not the end of understanding; it is the place where understanding begins to germinate into what Richard Rohr calls "endless knowability." Rohr focused on paradox in some devotions he wrote in 2016, and he summarized his points like this:

+ The binary, dualistic mind cannot deal with contradictions, paradox, or mystery, all of which are at the heart of religion.

+ The very nature of spiritual truth is that it is paradoxical.

+ The times where we meet or reckon with our contradictions are often turning points, opportunities to enter into the deeper mystery of God or, alternatively, to evade the mystery of God.

+ If you hold both sides seriously, that is the space in which you can grow morally, in understanding what really matters. That is the space in which you can go deep and learn mystery—which is endlessly [knowable].

+ The third way is not balancing or even eliminating the opposites, but holding the opposites, as Jesus did on the cross. To live inside this space of creative tension is the very character of faith, hope, and love.

+ [This third, Christ-like option] is overcoming seeming opposites by uncovering a reconciling third that is bigger than both of the parts and doesn't exclude either of them.[1]

Chesterton, as mentioned above, was driven by paradoxes, and an entire chapter in *Orthodoxy* is devoted to them. He begins the chapter by writing,

The real trouble with this world of ours is not that it is an unreasonable world, nor even that it is a reasonable one. The commonest kind of trouble is that it is nearly reasonable, but not quite. Life is not an illogicality; yet it is a trap for logicians. It looks just a little more mathematical and regular than it is; its exactitude is obvious, but its inexactitude is hidden; its wildness lies in wait. I give one coarse instance of what I mean. Suppose some mathematical creature from the moon were to reckon up the human body; he would at once see that the essential thing about it was that it was duplicate. A man is two men, he on the right exactly resembling him on the left. Having noted that there was an arm on the right and one on the left, a leg on the right and one on the left, he might go further and still find on each side the same number of fingers, the same number of toes, twin eyes, twin ears, twin nostrils, and even twin lobes of the brain. At last he would take it as a law; and then, where he found a heart on one side, would deduce that there was another heart on the other. And just then, where he most felt he was right, he would be wrong.[2]

Chesterton points out the essential need for paradox to understand even basic human reality—in this instance, a non-religious general and secular virtue like courage. He writes,

Granted that we have all to keep a balance, the real interest comes in with the question of how that balance can be kept. That was the problem which Paganism tried to solve: that was the problem which I think Christianity solved and solved in a very strange way. Paganism declared that virtue was in a balance; Christianity declared it was in a conflict: the collision of two passions apparently opposite. Of course they were not really inconsistent; but they were such that it was hard to hold simultaneously. Let us . . . take the case of courage. . . . Courage is almost a contradiction in terms. It means a strong desire to live taking the form of a readiness to die. "He that will lose his life, the same shall save it," is not a piece of mysticism for saints and heroes. It is a piece of everyday advice for sailors or mountaineers. It might be printed in an Alpine guide or a drill book. This paradox is the whole principle of courage; even of quite earthly or quite brutal courage. A man cut off by the sea may save his life if he will risk it on the precipice.[3]

For our purposes here, we need to connect Chesterton's ideas with the tensions of the four worldviews and the various lights in the chandelier. Paradox is not the seeming contradiction and the mysterious truth of a clever statement. Paradox is what happens when we find two polarities in reality that seem to be in conflict but both of them are true; thus, rather than picking one of the opposing truths and disregarding the other, we must hold both opposing truths in tension with each other. In my approach to worldview, I am not proposing some vague pluralism where all the views are simultaneously true and are actually one mushy "truth," which is not a truth at all. Nor am I saying that none of them are true. Rather, the fact is that materialism and idealism cannot both be true *in isolation of each other*. The key lies in paradox. Chesterton says that in Christianity, paradox "separated . . . two ideas and then exaggerated them both. In one way Man was to be haughtier than he had ever been before; in another way he was to be humbler than he had ever been before. In so far as I am Man I am the chief of creatures. In so far as I am *a* man I am the chief of sinners."[4] Chesterton concludes, "Here, again in short, Christianity got over the difficulty of combining furious opposites, by keeping them both, and keeping them both furious."[5]

If your head is spinning as you are reading this, that's okay! Let's consider Chesterton's courage example from above and put it more plainly here. If you do not care much about living and are willing to die, that requires no courage; the "readiness to die" is not balanced by "a strong desire to live," so there's no virtue in potentially giving up your life. And if you care so much about your life that you are not willing to die, you will also kill courage—you won't take the risk necessary to exhibit courage. Courage requires both a love for life and a willingness to die, and that is the key to paradox. Both truths are needed. You need to love living, but you must also be willing to die— even be willing to die so that someone else can live—if you want to be courageous. Once both of these aspects are part of the equation, the tension and truth of courage are achieved and sustained. Chesterton also unlocks the power of paradox by encouraging us to exaggerate the truths in opposite directions.

Watch what happens with courage. The more you love your life and the more you love living *and* the more you are willing to die and are ready to die for life and for others to live, the more your courage quotient grows.

Take the apostle Paul as an example. He did not want to die; he was on a mission from God to spread the Good News of the gospel of Christ to as many people as possible. But this mission was dangerous; he almost died several times and eventually *did* die because of his mission. Paul knew people wanted to kill him because of the message he was spreading, and he kept spreading it in the face of death. Yet Paul is the one who coined the phrase "To live is Christ and to die is gain" (Philippians 1:21, NIV). He knew death was nothing to be feared and heaven would be far better than his earthly existence; he knew God was in control of his life and death. Thus, he was not afraid to die; he was potentially even excited to die. He just did not *want* to die because he saw great purpose in his living. In light of this truth, one can see why he was so ferociously courageous! It disturbs me when people mock martyrs who die for what they believe, calling them into question for not leaving or running away, as if they were craving death. But true martyrs do not *want* to die; they are *willing* to die. They live with such hope and trust in their beliefs that they will turn those beliefs into courage in the face of death.

Let's examine what happens when we water down one of these truths or when we take one in isolation from the other paradoxical, balancing truth. If we do not think going to heaven after dying is gain, then we will hold tightly to life on earth. We will try to pack as much into it as possible, and we will be focused on satisfying ourselves in the here and now. We may fill our lives with meaningless junk and wasted hours of apathy or triteness. We will also be terrified of dying and will avoid anything that could cause us suffering. Now let's take the opposite: if we only live for heaven and do not see the power of living here and now for Christ, we will lose our purpose and meaning for getting out of bed each day in a world of persecution, suffering, and pain. We will lose our reason for interacting with others on a personal, relational, and material level.

When both a hope for eternity and a purpose and love for life are held in paradox, though, the result is stunning. When we believe that after physical death we will still have eternal life in a world that includes no suffering *and* we also believe that our life in the here and now has great purpose, then we can live and even thrive in the middle of suffering. In fact, we will even have the strength and hope and freedom to step into the suffering of others. When we hold both truths in tension and healthy opposition, we live with vigor and purpose, combined with freedom and hope, as we anticipate great reward and peace in eternal life after death. In the couplet that closes John Donne's poem "Death, be not proud," he speaks of the whimsy of paradox:

> *One short sleep past, we wake eternally*
> *And death shall be no more; Death thou shalt die.*[6]

I will indulge one more paradox—the Christian paradox of grace and works—to illustrate that both parts of the paradox must be life giving. Every semester in every class, I always have at least one student show up on day one of paradox training with these two sets of Bible verses to discuss the tension and legacy of this issue. Paul says in Ephesians 2:8-10,

> God saved you by his grace when you believed. And you can't take credit for this; it is a gift from God. Salvation is not a reward for the good things we have done, so none of us can boast about it. For we are God's masterpiece. He has created us anew in Christ Jesus, so we can do the good things he planned for us long ago.

And before I can say "paradox," the student inevitably quotes James 2:17-20:

> So you see, faith by itself isn't enough. Unless it produces good deeds, it is dead and useless.
> Now someone may argue, "Some people have faith; others have good deeds." But I say, "How can you show me your faith if you don't have good deeds? I will show you my faith by my good deeds."
> You say you have faith, for you believe that there is one God. Good for you! Even the demons believe this, and they tremble in terror. How foolish! Can't you see that faith without good deeds is useless?

Then they ask the question: "So is my salvation pure gift with no strings attached, no need for good deeds, or do I need to have good deeds for my faith to be real?" I always answer yes to that fantastic question. They are both true and both needed.

Let's deal with grace first. I am known for being a grace junkie. I am glad for that reputation. Now that I have tasted real grace, I am a fanatic: I teach about it a lot and come on strong, bold, and unashamed. Over and over I proclaim the truth that we can do nothing to earn our salvation either before *or after* we have accepted salvation by grace. Put your hands out like it is Christmas or your birthday, and let God drop salvation into your lap. You have been and are being saved by Christ. Will you accept and enjoy or resist and refuse this amazing gift? If we minimize grace and add any effort or "works" or a ritual like baptism or spiritual gifting like speaking in tongues, it ceases to be grace. Grace is a gift. We do nothing to earn it. We can only receive it, and then it's ours. It needs to be this way. Thus, all of our "works" or good deeds for God have been separated from our salvation by God. This is essentially *why* we are saved by grace: because it's all grace—no manipulation, behavior, attitude, fear, coercion, or anything else can be used to force or coerce us into receiving (or losing) our salvation. God in his infinite wisdom could have saved us by works or fear or command, but he chose grace because it makes our service and love freely given and it maintains our dignity. Because God saved us this way, our motivation to serve and love him is totally free and up to our discretion. In his letter to the Galatians, Paul is adamant about this. He firmly states, "It is for freedom that Christ has set us free. Stand firm, then, and do not let yourselves be burdened again by a yoke of slavery" (5:1, NIV). We can serve him or not serve him; our poor behavior, bad attitudes, or lack of intelligence, understanding, or good deeds will not negate our salvation. If it did, it would be our righteousness saving us, not Christ's. I tell people who have trusted in Christ to save them to imagine resting in the palm of God's very large hand. If God has promised to save those who trust in his ability to save, then saved they shall be. What thing is stronger than God that can take them or me out of his palm and keep us from being saved (see Romans 8:31-39)?

Nevertheless, knowing that our works do not save us, are we to do nothing for the God who has given us life and salvation? Far from it! Paul puts it mildly when he says our entire lives are to be living sacrifices for God (see Romans 12:1-2). God himself died for us to free us from death and sin. He offered himself as our righteousness as a pure gift. He forgives all our sins and imperfections. He gives us life and sustains our lives. With a God who has done and is doing all that—and more—who are we to give him only half our effort? Wouldn't a natural response to all this be to give him all we are, all we have? The other side of the coin is that none of our good deeds and hard work for God can make him love us more or save us more. In Christ, no sin (bad deed) will condemn any of us any longer, and no good deed can invoke more attention; he died and lives for all of us out of such unfathomable, endlessly outpouring love. This is where the paradox works its mysterious wonder. If we water down grace, we end up with only works and self-righteous behavior laced with fear and manipulation. And if we water down our works, we become apathetic to the God who saved us and made us and equipped us for good works; we miss out on our purpose; we serve only ourselves and in the process do ourselves a disservice because we were made to freely serve God. I do not want to miss out on the fullness of life that Christ offers me in serving him. Jesus says in John 10:10, "The thief comes only to steal and kill and destroy; I have come that they may have life, and have it to the full" (NIV). The best way to have life to the full is to work with all of our might for God. Both grace *and* works are needed, and needed in the extreme! The more we understand God's amazing grace, the more we want to serve him freely, motivated purely by love. The more we freely offer our lives in loving service to him, the more we understand the freedom and joy of his empowering grace and the less we miss out on the meaningful life offered to each of us.

If we water down either "side" (grace or works), we dip into heresy and the truth is lost. If you dig into Scripture, you will find a multitude of compelling and powerful verses that speak to the rich truths of grace *and* works. Yet I have seen churches overemphasize works and deemphasize grace or overemphasize grace and deemphasize works. The healthiest churches I have been a part of are grace junkies who freely and lovingly (and usually joyfully) work hard for Jesus and his Kingdom! This is a true, satisfying paradox. It is not a cop-out; it is a necessary surrender. Both are true, and each is in tension with the other. The key is to hold on to the tension, because when we try to resolve the tension of paradox, we lose the truth.

Not all paradoxes are satisfying, however. Some are very unsatisfying, and we need to be able to determine if a paradox satisfies or is simply meaningless, a never-ending vortex of thought. First, let me define what I mean by the word *satisfying*. *Satisfying* does not mean it can be completely understood, nor does it mean all tension and mystery are resolved; it simply means that it matches with our perceptions of reality in a way that is helpful and trustworthy. I trust the satisfying paradoxes; they are on my personal trust list. But the unsatisfying are not;

they are not worthy of my trust. For example, idealism has a paradox embedded within its answers to the question of what happens when you die. If you do not achieve oneness with the one perfect spiritual ideal, such as nirvana, you cease to exist (even with the idea of reincarnation, because you never reincarnate as the same person). Yet if perchance you do achieve oneness with the one (who is not you), then you *also* cease to exist because you only exist as the one, or you let go of self and achieve nirvana. Thus, the paradox is this: if you do not make it, you cease to exist, and if you make it, you cease to exist. The true Buddhists I've met have told me I am right on with this explanation, and they ask why I am not a Buddhist, since I understand it so well. They tell me that the goal of Buddhism is to achieve nothingness. I tell them that should not be too tough because, in essence, aren't they nothing already? A nice, quiet pause usually follows this, and then a mutual nod with some friendly smiles. We both understand each other.

A paradox of materialism asserts that we have a perception of free will but do not actually have free will. We have perceptions of meaning, but life is absurd. We have a desire for morality, but that desire is amoral and merely driven by chemical impulses. We are aware of our existence, but our existence is not objectively measurable.

Monism is similar in its hollow circularity. Authentic monists will assert that good and evil exist based on our perceptions and preferences, yet because good and evil are only perceptions, they are arbitrary and illusive and do not really exist. Pantheists will say we must wake up and achieve unity with god, but we must never forget that we already are god. The noblest truth of Hinduism is a paradox: "god dwells in me as me" ("I am that which I am looking for"). However, if god is me and I am god, then I simultaneously am not me and am god.

Although there are unsatisfying paradoxes, there are also satisfying ones—and these are life giving. This is a mystery, but we gain some understanding when we look at the paradox who is Jesus Christ. Christ holds all of reality in beautiful tension, in paradox. One of the central paradoxes has to do with the nature of reality, an idea we explored in part 2 of this text. We need Jesus to be fully God and fully man, fully spiritual and fully material. If you water down either of these realities, the essential truths are lost. But when our view of Christ encompasses and honors both spiritual and material reality, the truths from the four worldviews are found in one complete whole: Christ! In him all four "strips" of the painting are joined together: idealism's truth of the spiritual world and the perfect, objective ideal; materialism's truth of the physical world and the individualism and relativity of humans; monism's truth of the unity and connectedness of all things; and theism's truth of the relational distinction between God and humanity. All these truths are "held" in Christ. In him, all the lights of the chandelier are on. He is the image, the picture, the definition we need.

This text is specifically pointing toward Christ as the fullness of reality, and from a practical theistic perspective, nonmessianic Judaism and Islam cannot assert this type of paradoxical fullness of reality. There is no being, let alone human being, in these religions that ties all four of these fractured worldviews together like Jesus. Lewis writes, "Islam denies the Incarnation. It will not allow that God has descended into flesh or that Manhood has been exalted into Deity . . . It stands for all religions that are afraid of matter and afraid of mystery."[7] In no way am I deriding nonmessianic Judaism or Islam; I am simply stating one of the many key distinctions between them and a Christ-centered biblical worldview. It is short work at this point to see the lights on and lights off of these religions in regard to Jesus in this context of philosophy and paradox, especially when it comes to answering the question, who is God?

Like Chesterton, Lewis, Tolkien, and countless others, I have found that the journey and adventure of discovery that comes from learning about Christ is filled with hope, joy, freedom, and satisfaction particularly when I am using the powerful lens and tool of paradox. Simply look at an extensive name and character trait list used for God generated from Scripture, and you have a nice start: Jesus is Lion and Lamb, Beginning and End, Alpha and Omega, full of grace and truth, a Mighty Warrior and the Prince of Peace, to name just a few. I have found that most people, who write off complex theological or doctrinal issues and write off a relationship with Christ, often do so because of an unwillingness to explore, surrender to, accept, or even enjoy the mystery of paradox. Take a closer look, and you will find that most denominational divisions stem from a misunderstanding of paradox. This book explores what happens with humankind's view of reality when we do not accept paradox; we end up divided as seen in the *Last Supper* painting metaphor. What part of Christ or the Bible are you frustrated with, don't like, avoid, or have even rejected? If you do not trust or even hate God, what on your journey started that type of thinking? A quick look at C. S. Lewis's biography speaks to such a journey. Have you considered that this pain, frustration, or rejection may potentially originate from an unwillingness to accept, an attempt to resolve the tension of, or an unawareness of a profound paradox?

But how can Christ be *all*?

I believe the answer is found in the Trinity, in the three persons of God. Christ revealed God to be one God in three persons: Father, Son, and Spirit. This is the prime paradox of full reality: the three are one—are united—yet they are distinct. These three are in an everlasting relationship of love with each other that has no beginning and no end, in which there is mutual giving and receiving. For this reason, God *is* love: active, expressive, constant love. Theologians call the relationships between the persons of the Trinity the *perichoresis*, and many picture the perichoresis as an ongoing, beautiful dance. This dance is the Trinity's expression of love, and love flows from it in the creation of all that is, material and spiritual. The stars, the moon, you, me, peace, mountains, trees, hope, joy, rivers, giraffes, angels, babies, roly-poly bugs, family: all has been created—*is* being created—out of the love overflowing from a relationship of ceaseless love. And what was created in love was kept close; it was loved continually.

What went wrong with this? If this is what prompted creation, if created beings were in a continual relationship of love with their Creator and with each other, how are these relationships so broken today? How did we get to this state?

One of the overflowing gifts from the perichoresis is free will. The image of a dance helps us see the sense of this. Humanity was created with the choice to love or not love; to stay in relationship or leave it; to dance with God or not. Remember the last chapter, where we looked at our tendency to declare our own god, a god we can control, a god we can fully understand because he's our creation, because we've made god small and ourselves big? Humanity as a species has generally rejected God, and the beautiful Garden—in which all creation lived in perfect relationship with the Creator God—was ruined, and humans, separated from loving relationship with God, have been prone to create gods in our own image ever since. The God of love holds his hand out, inviting us to join in the dance of the Trinity on the dance floor of eternity, and we refuse. Ongoing and deepening division—between people and God, people and people, and people and nature—has been the result ever since. The Trinity in and as the fullness of reality dances on, and we stand by with our drinks and appetizer plates, watching, mocking, doubting, hiding in shame or fear—all in one way or another missing out.

Without relationship with God, humanity lost sight of God's standards of perfect love, goodness, and truth. Even when humans did catch glimpses of these standards, we found ourselves incapable of living by them. Humanity needed help, and God provided it. God provided God—in human form. Fully God, fully human, Christ came. He revealed to us the Father God we'd pushed away. He revealed the standard of perfect goodness and truth and love, and he met it. He disabled death and separation and sin with his own death and resurrection. He restored us to good standing with God. He shared his unifying Spirit with us, and with all this completed, he extended his loving hand to us in an invitation to join the dance of God.

In Jesus the Christ we have the fullness of all reality: material and spiritual, divine and human. In Christ we have light and beauty and goodness and truth. In Christ we have life—to the full.

Paradoxically, the culmination of a Christ-centered biblical worldview presented in this chapter is not the conclusion of this philosophy and worldview journey. Ironically, if the chapters in this text were to represent one's spiritual quest for truth, the real journey for truth has barely begun. As you will see in the following chapters, this entire text could be compared to a map loaded with various trails, and all of the previous chapters, like a map, have offered us only the capacity, the worldview, the vision, and the mind-set to take the first steps on the true journey *with* the Truth, not *for* the truth.

I close this chapter with a few more thoughts on how Jesus is the fullness of reality. Read these with a prayerful and contemplative heart as you come to understand the centrality of Christ Jesus to everything and particularly what it means to have Christ "in you" and to live, as Paul says, "in Christ."

We also pray that you will be strengthened with all his glorious power so you will have all the endurance and patience you need. May you be filled with joy, always thanking the Father. He has enabled you to share in the inheritance that belongs to his people, who live in the light. For he has rescued us from the kingdom of darkness and transferred us into the Kingdom of his dear Son, who purchased our freedom and forgave our sins.

Christ is the visible image of the invisible God.
   He existed before anything was created and is supreme over all creation,

for through him God created everything
    in the heavenly realms and on earth.
He made the things we can see
    and the things we can't see—
such as thrones, kingdoms, rulers, and authorities in the
    unseen world.
    Everything was created through him and for him.
He existed before anything else,
    and he holds all creation together.
Christ is also the head of the church,
    which is his body.
He is the beginning,
    supreme over all who rise from the dead.
    So he is first in everything.
For God in all his fullness
    was pleased to live in Christ,
and through him God reconciled
    everything to himself.
He made peace with everything in heaven and on earth
    by means of Christ's blood on the cross.

This includes you who were once far away from God.
You were his enemies, separated from him by your evil
thoughts and actions. Yet now he has reconciled you
to himself through the death of Christ in his physical
body. As a result, he has brought you into his own
presence, and you are holy and blameless as you stand
before him without a single fault.

COLOSSIANS 1:11-22

Gloria in Profundis

There has fallen on earth for a token
A god too great for the sky.
He has burst out of all things and broken
The bounds of eternity:
Into time and the terminal land
He has strayed like a thief or a lover,
For the wine of the world brims over,
Its splendour is spilt on the sand.

Who is proud when the heavens are humble,
Who mounts if the mountains fall,
If the fixed stars topple and tumble
And a deluge of love drowns all—
Who rears up his head for a crown,
Who holds up his will for a warrant,
Who strives with the starry torrent,
When all that is good goes down?

For in dread of such falling and failing
The fallen angels fell
Inverted in insolence, scaling
The hanging mountain of hell:
But unmeasured of plummet and rod
Too deep for their sight to scan,
Outrushing the fall of man
Is the height of the fall of God.

Glory to God in the Lowest
The spout of the stars in spate—
Where thunderbolt thinks to be slowest
And the lightning fears to be late:
As men dive for sunken gem
Pursuing, we hunt and hound it,
The fallen star has found it
In the cavern of Bethlehem.[8]

G. K. CHESTERTON

CHAPTER 21

The Treachery of Images

The myth became flesh. This is not a religion nor a philosophy;
it's the summing up and actuality of them all.
For this is the marriage of heaven and earth:
perfect Myth and perfect Fact;
claiming not only our love and obedience
but also our wonder and delight.

C. S. LEWIS

The Treachery of Images is a painting by the Belgian surrealist painter René Magritte. The painting is of a pipe. Below the pipe, Magritte painted the words *"Ceci n'est pas une pipe,"* French for "This is not a pipe."

Treachery is a betrayal of trust. I assert that for humans, there often is a treachery that leads to a misunderstanding related to our interpretation of reality—and theology and doctrine, for that matter. Truth is ultimately found in relationship with Christ, not in a list of trustworthy answers to big questions. The truth is not found in a book testifying about Jesus, even when the words are true. The truth is Christ himself. The picture of a pipe is not itself a pipe; it is a picture.

In a story in the Gospel of John, the Roman official Pilate

is face-to-face with the Truth. The arrested Jesus is standing in front of him, and Pilate asks the famous question: "What is truth?" (John 18:38). The Roman quest for truth was for an abstract concept, a set of ideas, the right string of words, a virtue. Pilate wants a definition of truth, such as a dictionary or an Internet search could provide. However, the answer, the Living God (the True Myth)—is standing right in front of him! John says the *Logos*—the "Word," Prime Reality—"became flesh" (John 1:14, NIV). The truth was incarnate—in the flesh. The Truth is right in front of Pilate; he can see Jesus, touch Jesus, hear Jesus. Yet he does not recognize or acknowledge Jesus Christ, God's Son, as the answer to his question. He asks, "*What* is truth?" not "*Who* is truth?" John records Jesus saying, "I am the way, the truth, and the life" (John 14:6). He does not say he will simply teach about the truth or write it down or show people where to find it. He says he *is* it.

Contrast Pilate's encounter with Jesus to Mary's encounter with Jesus just after he is resurrected (see John 20:16-18). Mary is a seeker, even to the point of seeking out the dead body of Jesus. Planning to mourn his death, she is instead amazed at his life. I love this story. When Mary ends up face-to-face with the Truth, she gives the Truth a bear hug—and then she becomes the first evangelist! That might be the perfect recipe for evangelism. Mary knows the difference between truth-as-concept and truth-as-person. "Jesus said to the people who believed in him, 'You are truly my disciples if you remain faithful to my teachings. And you will know the truth, and the truth will set you free'" (John 8:31-32). Mary was freed from demonic oppression by the Truth himself, not the concept of truth (see Luke 8:2). If she happened to be present when Jesus uttered this statement, she would know that Jesus' teachings were true, but the Truth that set her free was Jesus, not the teachings or the concept. We often interact with pictures of reality, texts about reality, or stories about reality and assume we have encountered the reality described in them. But this is not the case: we have encountered a picture, a book, or a story of reality, and these may very well reveal some of the reality or descriptions of truth to us, but they, in and of themselves, are not reality. C. S. Lewis put it like this:

> The books or the music in which we thought the
> beauty was located will betray us if we trust to them; it
> was not *in* them, it only came *through* them, and what
> came through them was longing. . . . For they are not
> the thing itself; they are only the scent of a flower we
> have not found, the echo of a tune we have not heard,
> news from a country we have never yet visited.[1]

I have taught philosophy to high school students for more than twenty years. As I share the four major worldviews and then move students toward a Christ-centered view of the world, I come back again and again to this concept. Each worldview is but a portion of the Truth, though we trust in our worldview and hold to it as if it were the whole. Yet I am convinced more and more deeply that even if we were able to put together the true pieces of all the worldviews, even if all the strips of the painting were reunited and all the lights of the chandelier were turned on, we would still only see the tenets of truth and the images of reality, but not truth and reality itself. The fullness of truth and reality is found only in the undivided Trinity embodied in the Christ. I know I just wrote this, but it is worth mentioning again in our highly academic and religiously saturated culture: Christ said that if we follow him and his teachings, we will know the truth and the truth will make us free (see John 8:31-32), but it is not our following or our believing the truths in the teachings or the sermons or the lessons that sets us free. It is not the right facts or premises or axioms, nor is it the right religion, doctrine, or theology, or even the right verses of Scripture. It is Christ himself. "If the Son sets you free," Jesus said, referring to himself, "you are truly free" (John 8:36). The Truth is God: the triune personhood of God found in the ideal spiritual reality of the Father; the material embodiment of the Son, Jesus Christ; and the unifying, life-giving wholeness of the powerful Holy Spirit of God.

In a letter written to the new church in Colossae (located in modern-day Turkey), the apostle Paul warned his readers not to be deceived by weak philosophy, bad doctrine, and shallow hearsay, which settles for strips of truth and does not pursue the fullness of truth. Paul speaks to this fullness in paradoxical language: "For in Christ lives all the fullness of God in a human body. So you also are complete through your union with Christ, who is the head over every ruler and authority" (Colossians 2:9-10).

Jesus himself calls out the religious people of his day when he draws this very distinct line between factual knowledge and relational knowledge. He says, "You search the Scriptures because you think they give you eternal life. But the Scriptures point to me! Yet you refuse to come to *me* to receive this life" (John 5:39-40, emphasis added).

As I read through the New Testament, I find that one of the

main messages, if not the main message, is a compelling invitation to trust that the person of Jesus Christ is the embodiment of the truth. He is truth incarnate—truth in the flesh. He is the one who will help us understand what is really real because *he* is really real.

This simple comparison might help connect the dots in what Jesus is saying about himself and what I am saying in this chapter. The book you are holding is filled with many of my words. Imagine my own children loving this book more than they love me. Imagine them quoting the book, studying the book, memorizing portions of the book, and yet never personally connecting with me. Imagine them telling others about the book and yet never building a loving relationship with me, the living author of the book, even though we live in the same house together.

As we come to the end of our exploration of philosophy and worldview, we need to make the leap from trusting information *about* the truth to trusting the living embodiment of truth, Jesus Christ. We need to go from trusting a list of statements *about* reality to trusting Christ, the fullness of reality.

This book is not an attempt to be "the truth." It is meant to point to the Truth. Just as René Magritte's painting of a pipe is not a pipe, a list of trustworthy truths is not the Truth. It is a list of truths about the Truth—the triune God: Father, Son, and Spirit. Nevertheless, a list of trustworthy sayings can point you to the living Truth who is worthy of your trust. Even as the apostle John was writing words about the Word himself—whom he knew personally, ate meals with, and loved—John knew his words were not the Word himself. His words point to the Word who became flesh, who dwelled awhile among us, and who is now seated at the right hand of the Father. His words point us to the Living God of the universe, who loves each of us as the beloved, a truth John knew well. He records Jesus speaking on this in his Gospel:

> I have loved you even as the Father has loved me. Remain in my love. When you obey my commandments, you remain in my love, just as I obey my Father's commandments and remain in his love. I have told you these things so that you will be filled with my joy. Yes, your joy will overflow! This is my commandment: Love each other in the same way I have loved you. There is no greater love than to lay down one's life for one's friends. You are my friends if you do what I command. I no longer call you slaves, because a master doesn't confide in his slaves. Now you are my friends, since I have told you everything the Father told me. You didn't choose me. I chose you. I appointed you to go and produce lasting fruit, so that the Father will give you whatever you ask for, using my name. This is my command: Love each other.
>
> JOHN 15:9-17

A few verses later, John's words point to the Spirit, who dwelled in Jesus while he was on earth and who now also dwells in us. This is the Spirit Jesus promised us before he returned to the Father. Who else would give us life to the full but the life-giving Spirit of Christ dwelling in each of us, not as us, but distinct from us and making us more and more "us" while simultaneously shaping us into the image of our loving Creator?

The four trust lists used in this book point us to a person, to the person of Christ, to the Truth as the living, incarnate, fullness of reality. Philosophy in this book has been used as a tool, a means to an end—and that end is Christ.

CHAPTER 22

The Road Goes Ever On and On

The Road goes ever on and on
Down from the door where it began.
Now far ahead the Road has gone,
And I must follow, if I can,
Pursuing it with weary feet,
Until it joins some larger way,
Where many paths and errands meet.
And whither then? I cannot say.

J. R. R. TOLKIEN

Many blessings to you on your personal quest to know the Truth, to be loved, and to love.

Understanding divine love as motivation and a guide to robustly live is the culmination of this entire text, and it is the starting point and foundation for the rest of the journey. Scripture says that trusting (believing) in Christ saves. Trusting in Christ is one thing; becoming a dedicated follower, a disciple of Christ, is another. We are not adequately prepared to follow Jesus and trust him more fully as authentic disciples until we have realized his openhanded, openhearted love for us. This text offers you a

Christ-centered worldview that allows for and invites you into a grace-filled, loving relationship with Christ. The next book in this series, *Inklings on Christ-Centered Biblical Discipleship*, is an invitation to *use* this Christ-centered worldview to live your life in the "true myth" as an authentic disciple of Jesus. Discipleship simply isn't sustainable without a Christ-centered worldview, which is why this text comes first. But as with *The Treachery of Images*, don't mistake the first step—having a Christ-centered worldview—for the destination, a life lived in loving relationship with Jesus Christ. Don't mistake orthodoxy (right thinking) for orthopraxy (right practice); both are essential.

The final word for you is simply to remember that we are *all* on a journey, each of us. Stories of other people's journeys, introduced to us through literature and history, teach that there are often not straight paths with mile markers regularly spaced along the way. Rather, our paths are filled with trials and triumphs, sorrows and joys, despair and hope. We must remember that each person is at a different place and stage along their journey, unique to them. In Tolkien's epic Lord of the Rings series, Gandalf offers Frodo some timeless encouragement as he begins his journey. Frodo asks, "Why was I chosen?" And Gandalf replies, "You may be sure that it was not for any merit that others do not possess: not for power or wisdom, at any rate. But you have been chosen, and you must therefore use such strength and heart and wits as you have."[1]

Gandalf's powerful declaration echoes the words that Jesus affirmed to an expert in religious law as *the* path to life: "'You must love the Lord your God with all your heart, all your soul, all your strength, and all your mind.' And, 'Love your neighbor as yourself'" (Luke 10:27).

Can you lovingly help someone move to the next stage of his or her journey? How can you equip or empower someone with the courage to take one more step? This is an essential component of a loving community. We can honor the process of each person's individual journey. We can learn to truly love God (not just the concept of God), we can continually grow in genuine love for each other, we can learn to really love ourselves (as God loves us), and we can freely extend grace to all.

These last chapters have been a direct invitation to seek and to know Christ, with the encouragement that if you choose to do so, you *will* find Christ. God says, "If you look for me wholeheartedly, you will find me" (Jeremiah 29:13), and Jesus promises, "Keep on asking, and you will receive what you ask for. Keep on seeking, and you will find. Keep on knocking, and the door will be opened to you" (Matthew 7:7). You will not have to go far to find him. In fact, he already has been seeking you and will continue to do so. Furthermore, this journey does not need to end because there is infinitely more of Christ's love to receive, to experience, and to share, especially for those who accept his bold invitation to the life-long adventure of discipleship. We can have confidence and enduring hope that the King who has come is still with us and is establishing his Kingdom *here* and *now*. Ultimately, the fullness of his Kingdom is coming, and his glorious Kingdom has no end.

> "Look! I stand at the door and knock. If you hear my voice and open the door, I will come in, and we will share a meal together as friends."
> REVELATION 3:20

HONOR &
ACKNOWLEDGMENTS

This book would not exist without the massive encouragement, support, expertise, and sacrifice of so many people, the first of whom is my wife, Jennifer Dominguez, an excellent writer and editor and a true friend. My children—Anna, Elijah, Olivia, and Ivy—and my faithful yellow labs quickly fall in line after her. "It is not often that someone comes along who is a true friend and a good writer" (E. B. White, *Charlotte's Web*).

I owe a special thank-you to Jen Underwood. Without your initial editorial prowess, this book would have been twice as long, unreadable, and unfinished. It was a joy to create with you.

To Jonathan, my main editor at Tyndale: I am convinced that God connected us for such a time as this, like Gandalf and Aragorn. "Truth, like gold, is to be obtained not by its growth, but by washing away from it all that is not gold" (Leo Tolstoy).

Thank you to *all* of my wonderful, crazy, awesome family and friends who have been and continue to be on this beautiful adventure.

Thank you, Chris Grant and Chris Browne, for your friendship and vision in getting this manuscript started!

Thank you, Bob Smalley, for being a Tom Bombadil, and

Charles Bressler for being a Gandalf, so many years ago at Houghton College.

Thank you to all of the amazing and resourceful staff at the Marion E. Wade Center at Wheaton College. Laura and Elaine, your soothing graciousness and quiet stewardship embody the aroma of Lothlórien and the strength of Minas Tirith.

Thank you to Chris Mitchel, Jerry Root, Mark Neal, and the "Brotherhood of the Briar," "Poetry, Pints, and Prophecy," and the "Quill and Ink Society."

Thank you, again, Chris Grant, for the inspiration, the motivation, all of the breakfasts, and The Perch. Thank you for vision and structure and for "thirty minutes a day and four-hour chunks!"

Thank you, Captain Redbeard! "I will drink Life to the lees. . . . That which we are, we are—One equal-temper of heroic hearts . . . strong in will—To strive, to seek, to find, and not to yield."

Thank you, Andrew Hopson: "The moon is up over One Tree Hill. . . ."

Thank you, Jack Burgess: "O for a Muse of fire . . ."

Thank you, Nate Leman: "We few, we happy few . . ." Tilly (aka Galadriel) and Sean (aka "Mr. Beard" and "Gimli")—the fellowship and the epic adventure would not be the same without you. I am eternally grateful.

Sweet Trish Main: "I can no other answer make but thanks, And thanks . . ." A thousand times, thanks.

Thank you, Steve Berger, for your perpetual and timely encouragement.

Thank you, Brother Bob, for being a Samwise Gamgee and for the crack-of-dawn fellowship and prayer.

Thank you to Chip Huber for continually inviting me "further up and further in."

Thank you, Captain Scott Souders, Navigator Matt Molenhouse, Lieutenant Joel Visker, Commodore Leigh Mikolajczyk, Colton Seager, David Aulie, Kenny Hass, Kipper Wagner, Adam Ghosh, Josiah Campbell, and all of the crews from AUP for helping me step out of the boat!

Thank you, Tonya Westervelt, for your close reading, critical eye, wit, insight, and candor. It is an honor to adventure with your entire family.

Thank you, Joe Timmer, Luke Regan, Kevin Elkin, Ben Varner, and sweet Maddie Hazel for your camaraderie and encouragement. "Once more to the breach, dear friends, once more . . ."

Thank you, Micah Trautwein, for your countless sacrificial hours of transcription; without your persistence I would not have gained the traction needed to move forward with the original manuscript.

Thank you, Paul Mouw, for your Kingdom wisdom and insight.

Thank you to Mark and Amy Wilson for your magnanimous kindness and benevolent hospitality. I will never forget the fellowship, the walks in the woods, and the days writing in the community kitchen and little cabin in Hancock, New Hampshire.

Thank you, Sue and Frank Smolinkski and Babsyboo and Dave Seely: your Kingdom hearts of unconditional love, powerful encouragement, and openhanded generosity naturally echo Rivendell in countless ways.

Thank you to Luz Vergara and the powerful and loving WA Moms Prayer Group.

Thank you to twenty-five years of amazing, engaged Kingdom students and inspiring Kingdom colleagues!

Thank you to U2, David Crowder, Mumford & Sons, Rend Collective, Josh Garrels, Hillsong, Bethel Music, Andrew Peterson, and Cody Martin for the inspiration, the soundtrack, and the Presence.

Thank you to Chuck Parry for mentoring me and sharing your Christ-centered biblical view of the world with me and my family, for personally modeling the authentic discipleship journey, for *Free Falling*, and for bringing the Gospels and the book of Acts alive.

Thank you, Danny Silk, for *Culture of Honor*.

Thank you, Emily Mason, for your precise words of life about this book and project.

Thank you, Wendell Berry, for inspiring me to "practice resurrection."

Thank you, Richard Rohr, for the BIG VISION, for a tone of relaxed honor, for the invitation to embrace the Mystery and Paradox, for the Shalom, and for *Adam's Return*.

Thank you, Henri Nouwen, for *Return of the Prodigal Son* and *Life of the Beloved* and for some of my first glimpses of the Kingdom come.

I am eternally grateful to Chesterton, Lewis, and Tolkien for their life, legacy, words, and vision.

Thank you to Linda Howard and the amazing team—family— at Tyndale for investing in this adventure and for working your magic! Shout-out to Jen Phelps: you are a brilliant artist.

Thank you, Jesus, for your enduring patience, love, and grace.

Thank *you* for reading this book and sharing in this grand adventure!

When I think of all this, I fall to my knees and pray to the Father, the Creator of everything in heaven and on earth. I pray that from his glorious, unlimited resources he will empower you with inner strength through his Spirit. Then Christ will make his home in your hearts as you trust in him. Your roots will grow down into God's love and keep you strong. And may you have the power to understand, as all God's people should, how wide, how long, how high, and how deep his love is. May you experience the love of Christ, though it is too great to understand fully. Then you will be made complete with all the fullness of life and power that comes from God.

Now all glory to God, who is able, through his mighty power at work within us, to accomplish infinitely more than we might ask or think. Glory to him in the church and in Christ Jesus through all generations forever and ever! Amen.

EPHESIANS 3:14-21

NOTES

INTRODUCTION

1. Erwin McManus, "Ep 022: Erwin McManus," *The Global Leadership Summit Podcast*, podcast audio, March 19, 2018, https://globalleadership.org/podcast/leading-organizations/ep-022-erwin-mcmanus/.
2. McManus, "Ep 022: Erwin McManus."
3. Augustine, *On Christian Doctrine*, trans. J. F. Shaw (Mineola, NY: Dover Publications, 2009), 53.
4. G. K. Chesterton, *Orthodoxy* (New York: Doubleday, 1908), 44.
5. C. S. Lewis, *The Collected Letters of C. S. Lewis, Volume 2: Books, Broadcasts, and the War, 1931–1949*, ed. Walter Hooper (New York: HarperSanFrancisco, 2004), 1.
6. Alfred, Lord Tennyson, "Ulysses," Poetry Foundation, accessed June 25, 2019, https://www.poetryfoundation.org/poems/45392/ulysses.

CHAPTER 2: FAITH AND FAITH ISLAND

1. G. K. Chesterton, *Orthodoxy* (New York: Doubleday, 1908), 33.
2. *Inception*, directed by Christopher Nolan, performed by Leonardo DiCaprio, Joseph Gordon-Levitt, and Ellen Page (Burbank, CA: Warner Bros., 2011).

CHAPTER 3: TRUST LISTS: THE CONCEPT AND THE TOOL

1. William Shakespeare, *The Tragedy of Hamlet Prince of Denmark*, ed. Bernice W. Kliman and James H. Lake (Indianapolis: Focus, 2008), 70.

CHAPTER 4: THE SUICIDE OF THOUGHT
1. G. K. Chesterton, *Orthodoxy* (New York: Doubleday, 1908), 33.
2. G. K. Chesterton, "The Suicide of Thought," in *Orthodoxy* (New York: Doubleday, 1908), 30–45.
3. Chesterton, 44.
4. Chesterton, 37.
5. Richard Rohr, "Universal Reality," Center for Action and Contemplation, April 21, 2016, https://cac.org/universal-reality-2016-04-21/.
6. C. S. Lewis, *Mere Christianity* (New York: HarperCollins, 2015), 47–48.

CHAPTER 6: PHILOSOPHY: A PRACTICAL TOOL
1. G. K. Chesterton, *Orthodoxy* (Colorado Springs: Shaw Books, 2001), vii.
2. Chesterton, xii.
3. Anne Frank, *Anne Frank's Tales from the Secret Annex: A Collection of Her Short Stories, Fables, and Lesser-Known Writings*, ed. Gerrold van der Stroom and Susan Massotty (New York: Bantam, 2003), 121.

CHAPTER 7: THE POWER OF A QUESTION
1. James Sire, *The Universe Next Door* (Downers Grove, IL: InterVarsity Press, 2009), 22–23.
2. Sire, 80.
3. Sire, 43.

CHAPTER 9: A CLOSER LOOK AT AUTHENTIC MATERIALISM
1. *Planet Earth*, Season 1, Episode 7, "Great Plains," directed by Alastair Fothergill, aired November 12, 2006, on BBC.
2. W. H. Auden, "The Fall of Rome," Poets.org, accessed June 27, 2019, https://poets.org/poem/fall-rome.
3. James Sire, *The Universe Next Door* (Downers Grove, IL: InterVarsity Press, 2009), 119.

CHAPTER 11: A CLOSER LOOK AT RELIGIOUS THEISM
1. C. S. Lewis, *Mere Christianity* (New York: HarperCollins, 2015), 47–48.
2. James Sire, *The Universe Next Door* (Downers Grove, IL: InterVarsity Press, 2009), 43.

CHAPTER 13: OPEN OUR EYES SO WE CAN SEE
1. Andrea A. Lunsford, *The Presence of Others: Voices and Images that Call for Responses*, 3rd ed. (Boston: Bedford/St. Martin's, 2000), 467.

2. *The Dialogues of Plato*, Great Books of the Western World, vol. 7 (Encyclopaedia Britannica, 1952), 389.
3. Lunsford, *The Presence of Others*, 467.
4. G. K. Chesterton, *Orthodoxy* (New York: Doubleday, 1908), 44.

CHAPTER 14: CONNECTING TRUTH

1. My dear friend and gifted art history teacher Nate Leman has helped me develop this metaphor and even has adopted it as the final exam in his class. He has shown me how enlightening it is to uncover the truth that all great art has the capacity to do collectively what I have done with this one painting. I will say later that all great stories point to the true Great Story; he posits that all great art points us to the True Great Artist.
2. C. S. Lewis, *Mere Christianity* (New York: HarperCollins, 2015), 35.

CHAPTER 15: THE LIGHT OF THE WORLD

1. I developed this metaphor with my good friend and colleague Jack Burgess.
2. Ultimately, in this metaphor, Christ would also be the electricity/flame that gives the individual lights their brilliance.
3. William Shakespeare, *Shakespeare's Twelfth Night: With Notes, Examination Papers, and Plan of Preparation* (London: W. and R. Chambers, 1895), 67.

CHAPTER 16: IDEALISM: LIGHTS ON AND OFF

1. C. S. Lewis, *Mere Christianity* (New York: HarperCollins, 2015), 56–57.

CHAPTER 17: MATERIALISM: LIGHTS ON AND OFF

1. Daniel Menaker, "Have It Your Way: 'Free Will,' by Sam Harris," *New York Times*, July 13, 2012, https://www.nytimes.com/2012/07/15/books/review /free-will-by-sam-harris.html.
2. C. S. Lewis, *Mere Christianity* (New York: HarperCollins, 2015), 38–39.

CHAPTER 18: MONISM: LIGHTS ON AND OFF

1. The apostle Paul refers to this as the "mystery of Christ." Without jumping too far ahead, it is important to note the difference between being united "*in* Christ" and "*by* Christ" or "*by* God" versus united "*as* Christ" or "*as* God."
2. *Star Wars: Episode III—Revenge of the Sith*, directed by George Lucas, performed by Hayden Christensen, Natalie Portman, and Ewan McGregor (San Francisco: Lucasfilm, 2005).
3. G. K. Chesterton, *Orthodoxy* (New York: Doubleday, 1908), 36–37.

CHAPTER 19: RELIGIOUS THEISM: LIGHTS ON AND OFF

1. C. S. Lewis, *Mere Christianity* (New York: HarperCollins, 2015), 9, 26.
2. Paradoxically, because our view of God is the most important influence in shaping who we are (see A. W. Tozer epigraph on page 99), humans need to understand who God has revealed himself to be. God needs to speak for himself about who he is. Thus, we have various religious texts that claim to be the revelation of God to man and, thus, various texts for our various trust lists. However, these religious texts do not all align regarding the character and nature of God, and some are even diametrically opposed to each other. Consequently, Christians need the Bible to be a firm foundation with clear boundaries regarding who God is and who God is not. The Bible will be on their trust lists. Therefore, I am not just offering a Christ-centered worldview in this text but rather a Christ-centered biblical worldview.

CHAPTER 20: THE POWER OF PARADOX

1. Richard Rohr, "Paradox," Center for Action and Contemplation, August 27, 2016, https://cac.org/paradox-weekly-summary-2016-08-27/.
2. G. K. Chesterton, *Orthodoxy* (New York: Doubleday, 1908), 81.
3. Chesterton, 92–93.
4. Chesterton, 94.
5. Chesterton, 95.
6. John Donne, "Holy Sonnets: Death, Be Not Proud," Poetry Foundation, accessed July 1, 2019, https://www.poetryfoundation.org/poems/44107/holy-sonnets-death-be-not-proud.
7. Wayne Martindale and Jerry Root, eds., *The Quotable Lewis* (Carol Stream, IL: Tyndale, 1990), 621.
8. G. K. Chesterton, "Gloria in Profundis," The Apostolate of Common Sense, The Society of Gilbert Keith Chesterton, accessed July 1, 2019, https://www.chesterton.org/gloria-in-profundis/.

CHAPTER 21: THE TREACHERY OF IMAGES

1. C. S. Lewis, *The Weight of Glory* (New York: HarperCollins, 2001), 30–31.

CHAPTER 22: THE ROAD GOES EVER ON AND ON

1. J. R. R. Tolkien, *The Fellowship of the Ring* (Boston: Houghton Mifflin, 1988), 70.